Living Torah

Living Torah

Gateway to a Timeless Tradition

Gil Graff
Foreword by Rabbi David Wolpe

ROWMAN & LITTLEFIELD
Lanham • Boulder • New York • London

Published by Rowman & Littlefield
An imprint of The Rowman & Littlefield Publishing Group, Inc.
4501 Forbes Boulevard, Suite 200, Lanham, Maryland 20706
www.rowman.com

86-90 Paul Street, London EC2A 4NE

British Library Cataloguing in Publication Information Available

Library of Congress Cataloging-in-Publication Data Available

ISBN 9781538194294 (cloth: alk. paper) | ISBN 9781538194300 (ebook)

♾™ The paper used in this publication meets the minimum requirements of American National Standard for Information Sciences—Permanence of Paper for Printed Library Materials, ANSI/NISO Z39.48-1992.

Contents

Preface and Acknowledgments

I was privileged to know my father's parents who immigrated to the United States, in 1912, as newlyweds. I have also been privileged to interact with grandchildren, the eldest of whom was born in 2017. The world of my grandparents and the world of my grandchildren is dramatically different. Over the intervening generations, two world wars; the annihilation of most of European Jewry as part of a systematic, state-sponsored campaign of genocide; the rise and fall of the USSR; the establishment of a sovereign Jewish state in Israel and its extraordinary development; and the growth and flourishing of American Jewry are but some of the global events that have had profound impacts on world history and Jewish life.

The airplane, mass production of automobiles, space travel, computers, the internet, cell phones, and remarkable discoveries in medicine and medical treatment are among the advances of science and technology dating from the start of the twentieth century. Notwithstanding such significant changes, people today, as throughout the ages, reflect on how best to live during the limited years of our earthly existence. For Jews, the Torah, as interpreted and applied over the course of millennia, has served as an enduring guide to leading a purposeful life.

My Yiddish-speaking paternal grandparents left Eastern Europe for Palestine, then part of the Ottoman Empire; they met in Petah Tikvah, where both had settled. In search of improved economic opportunity, they, as millions of immigrants—then, as now—made their way to America. My grandfather launched a scrap metal business, starting, independently, with a horse and wagon and "graduating," over time, to trucks and an expanded workforce, including two sons (at various times), a son-in-law, and several employees. The Graff home was known to be hospitable and attentive to Jewish dietary laws, and my grandparents' six children, born 1913–1928, recalled being displaced from their beds to accommodate visitors who would suddenly appear, having been advised that the Graff home was a place at which they would be welcomed, and where the food was reliably kosher.

Though lacking substantial, formal education, my grandparents were steeped in Jewish tradition and were fully conversant with the text of the Torah as well as many traditional commentaries on the Torah. My grandmother, known for her piety, read *Ze'na u-Re'ena*, a Yiddish work, written especially for women, that included exegetical interpretations of the weekly Torah portion. My grandfather did not consider himself well learned, but he often quoted passages from classical rabbinic literature that related to the Torah text. The study and practice of Torah were, organically, part of their lives.

Their American-born children attended public schools as well as after-school Talmud Torah (literally, "study of Torah," referring, in this case, to part-time Jewish education) classes. Talmud Torah programs, in that generation, often met ten to twelve hours per week, Monday through Thursday afternoons or evenings, and Sunday morning. My father and one of his brothers (as well as a brother-in-law) were among the sixteen million Americans who served in the United States military during World War II and benefited from the postwar opportunities afforded by the GI bill.

Both Graff veterans earned a doctorate in their respective fields. My father's professional career was as a physicist; my uncle was a psychologist. Both men took, and my father continues to take, great interest in Torah study and the implications and applications of Torah to contemporary society. Their siblings, too, maintained lifelong interest in the Torah and many of the themes explored in this book.

I am part of the post–World War II "baby boom" generation, born in Los Angeles, a city that experienced explosive growth in the postwar decades. As baby boomers came of age, a search for meaning was palpable. The civil rights movement, feminism, and burgeoning interest in ethnic studies (including Jewish studies) were integral to the landscape of the 1960s and 1970s. Interest in purposeful living made Torah study all the more relevant to those ready to engage in it.

As a high school and university student in the late 1960s and 1970s, I experienced the opportunity of studying Jewish texts with a number of outstanding individuals of diverse backgrounds and perspectives. Among those teachers were Rabbi Yosef Blau, long-serving *mashgiach ruchani* (spiritual mentor) at the Rabbi Isaac Elchanan Theological Seminary (RIETS), with whom I studied when he taught at Hebrew Theological College, in Chicago; Rabbi Dr. Moshe Davidowitz (known, after moving to Israel—where, among other things, he directed the Jewish Futures Network—as Moshe Dror), with whom I studied at Spertus College of Judaica (now Spertus Institute for Jewish Learning and Leadership); Rabbi Dr. Elliot Dorff, rector and professor of Jewish philosophy at American Jewish University, with whom I studied Jewish law—and its roots in biblical and rabbinic texts—at UCLA School of Law; Professor Amos Funkenstein, a scholar with immense breadth and depth of Jewish learning who was my teacher and dissertation advisor at UCLA; Dr. Nehama Leibowitz, professor of biblical commentaries and Torah educator par excellence, with whom I was privileged to study at Hebrew University, in Jerusalem; and Rabbi Dr. David Lieber, longtime professor of Bible and president of the University of Judaism (now American Jewish University) and editor of the *Etz Hayim* Torah commentary, whose courses on books of the Hebrew Bible I sought out at UCLA's Department of Near Eastern Languages.

During those formative years of study, there was a particular encounter that underscored my sense that engaging with Jewish texts is an essential aspect of understanding and experiencing Jewishness and Judaism. The setting was a course in Jewish philosophy, at Hebrew University. While exploring an important twentieth-century work by Martin Buber, *I and Thou*, the instructor, Rivka Horowitz, invited another twentieth-century Jewish thinker, who was visiting Jerusalem, to address the class. That guest was Rabbi Mordecai Kaplan (1881–1983), who—at age ninety years—remained sharp as a tack. Kaplan came to class with a clearly well-used *TaNaKh* (Hebrew Bible) in hand. He flipped to various passages and asked the assembled students to explain the texts to which he turned. We were individually and collectively only vaguely familiar with most of the passages to which he directed our attention.

Rabbi Kaplan left us with the takeaway that anyone who thinks to meaningfully philosophize about or construct or reconstruct a vital

Judaism must begin with grounding in classical Jewish texts. It was a message that I immediately applied by devoting further study to such texts, before embarking on the road to a PhD in Jewish history. Engaging with classical Jewish texts, starting with the Torah—which is "serialized" in weekly installments, read aloud at synagogues throughout the world, and completed, beginning to end, each year—is a lifelong journey.

In the early decades of the twenty-first century, the pace of change has become ever more rapid. In recent years, humanity encountered a pandemic that took millions of lives. Beyond that, the challenges of contemporary times—from incessant, regional warfare, to global warming, escalating social and political polarization, and more—are substantial. Amid all of this, the light that the Torah can provide is considerable, but many are unaware that this is so.

On that backdrop, I acknowledge with appreciation my indebtedness to family members who, by example and by the provision of learning opportunities, introduced me to "living Torah," that is, Torah as a way of life and Torah as a dynamic work. My parents, Chaim and Senta Graff, and grandparents, Sol and Minnie Graff, did much to introduce me to this family heritage. My father's siblings—three brothers and two sisters—and their spouses, whom I came to know during my years of high school and college study in Chicago, modeled in their own ways the influence of Torah teachings.

I have gained much from outstanding teachers, including but by no means limited to the previously referenced educators and scholars. That I was privileged to study at institutions of higher Jewish learning in the United States and Israel—together home to 85 percent of world Jewry—is a gift that would not have been imagined at the time of my grandparents' birth. I express thanks to the students in many settings, including the Academy for Jewish Religion California, American Jewish University, Hebrew Union College-Jewish Institute of Religion, Spertus Institute for Jewish Learning and Leadership, and Touro College, who raised questions, shared insights and ideas, stimulated my thinking, and inspired me to write this book.

For nearly four decades, I have worked at an organization in greater Los Angeles whose mission it is to educate successive generations of Jews toward knowledge, understanding, appreciation, and internalization of their heritage. Interactions with students, educators, parents, and volunteers through my work at Builders of Jewish Education (BJE) contributed significantly to the development of this volume. I am particularly grateful to my colleagues on the staff of BJE and the dedicated board leaders of this vital educational agency.

This book benefited from the review of earlier drafts by Michael Berenbaum, PhD; Elaine Goodfriend, PhD; Bennett L. Spiegel, Esq.; and Rabbi David Wolpe and the comments of several anonymous readers on sections of the work, for which I am appreciative. My thanks as well to David Nimmer, Esq., for his advice and counsel. I express my gratitude to Rabbi Wolpe for generously writing a foreword to this volume. I am indebted to Richard Brown, PhD, senior executive religion editor at Rowman & Littlefield, for his embrace of this project, close review and comments on an earlier draft, and steadfast support in bringing the book to print; thanks, also, to assistant editor Victoria Shi for her assistance along the way. Special thanks to Chen Bain and Talia Graff for their technical support in preparing the manuscript for publication.

My greatest thanks are to my wife, Robin, a longtime Jewish educator, who shares an abiding interest in Torah and is my partner in Jewish learning and living. Our children, from whom I have learned and continue to learn a great deal, and their spouses and children are legatees of a Torah-grounded heritage that has guided their family and, more broadly, the Jewish people—and influenced much of humanity—for millennia. With deep appreciation, I gratefully acknowledge the Torah (literally, instruction) as understood, lived, and transmitted by generations past. It is to next generations, those already born and those yet unborn, that this volume is dedicated. It is my hope that my grandchildren, Rafael Jacob, Leo Jonah, and Azriel Gil, will, as their great-great grandparents who came to American shores in 1912, be rooted and find meaning in the timeless teachings of Torah and convey that legacy to those who follow.

Foreword

Rabbi David Wolpe

The Bible is at once a contender for the most read and most misunderstood book of all time. So many have poured their preconceptions and aspirations into its pages that the reader who approaches it hoping to understand what it is actually about faces a challenge. There are annotated Bibles, abridged Bibles, every form and shape and substance of this most important of texts.

The Torah, which is the core of the Bible, contains stories that most of us are at least vaguely familiar with: Adam and Eve, the liberation of the Israelites from Egypt, the golden calf, and more. Yet, when we actually read these stories, they are often different from our recollection, almost like when we return to a childhood home and find it is very different from our memory of it. They are subtler, richer, and hold more wisdom than we remembered. A classic is a book that grows as we do, and there is no book more classic than the Torah.

Any book about a book is a selection. If one were to tell the entire story of the Torah, all you would need to do is recopy the Torah! Yet here is where the lens of centuries is helpful rather than obscuring. In the hands of a master teacher, a book about the Torah can give you the major ideas, themes, and personalities of the Torah in an elegant and accessible style. You see the edifice take shape and it all makes sense.

Such a project is dependent on the teacher of course. Here I can speak with both knowledge and confidence. Nearly a half-century ago, when I first arrived in California at the age of eighteen to work at Camp Ramah in California, the first new friends I made were Gil and

Robin Graff. They were not only friends; they opened their home to me (I stayed there for weeks), and I learned from them from the first moments we met.

Gil Graff has, for years, directed the central Jewish educational agency on the West Coast. He does not merely teach; he teaches the teachers. In a lifetime of teaching and learning, he understands as well as anyone the themes of the Torah that not only illustrate the book itself but thread through the lives of modern readers. In short, this is a book about the Torah that will not only teach you about the Torah, it will also teach you about the struggles, themes, and meaning of your own life.

You are reading right now—what is the significance of the fact that Jews were expected to be able to read? It may surprise you, although you will learn it in this book—that such a skill was very rare in most cultures. Why does the Torah have very specific, seemingly superfluous lines such as, "you shall not put a stumbling block before the blind?" Who would imagine doing such a thing? Do we really need a law telling us not to do that? But I will bet you, once you understand what that line really means, that you will be able to think of an example from the last month in your own life when you or someone close to you violated that prohibition.

How to summarize the book you hold in your hands? It is a distillation of thousands of years of wisdom about the wisest of texts. You will learn some history, to be sure. But the essence of this book is not the history or the religious practices that form part of the overall picture of the Torah. The essence is learning the themes of what Gil himself tells us in the introduction: "a connection to Israel, the Jews in history, ritual, community, and Jewish study. These themes, individually and collectively, can be sources of meaning for Jews living in the twenty-first century."

You don't only hold a book in your hands—you hold a gateway. Like the gateway leading to that childhood home, this is your legacy and your memory. But it is also your guide, and our future. As the great Rabbi Hillel said—go and learn.

—Rabbi David Wolpe

Introduction

My work on this volume spanned three years during which the world experienced a pandemic. Soon after I completed an initial draft, on a Jewish holiday during which an annual cycle of Torah study concludes and starts anew, 1,200 people were brutally murdered in Israel, and more than 240 people were seized as hostages by thousands of well-organized terrorists who invaded from neighboring Gaza. Israel responded with a vigorous military campaign aimed at freeing the kidnapped hostages and dismantling the military capability of Hamas, which had controlled Gaza since 2007 and carried out the murders and abductions of October 7, 2023.

The conditions of life are dynamic and unpredictable. Whether amid a pandemic, war, or more "ordinary" times, the significance of the Torah and its themes is enduring. The Torah is the cornerstone of an intergenerational Jewish conversation; it connects Jews across time and place. This book is a gateway to the timeless wisdom of Torah.

The most recent 150 years have arguably been no less transformative in the experience of the Jewish people than the period from 70 to 220 CE. Early in the first millennium of the Common Era the Second Temple was destroyed, a Judean Revolt (Bar Kochba War) against Rome was quashed, the Mishnah—an organized collection of oral traditions on far-ranging facets of Jewish law—was redacted, and Judea's native population declined such that it was no longer the demographic center of Jewish life. Fast forward to the nineteenth century, and Jews' encounter with modernity gave rise to new approaches to and expressions of Judaism as well as a movement to reclaim Jewish nationality; migration patterns led to significant shifts in Jewish population centers.

Rather than functioning as a corporate community, Jews, increasingly, became individual citizens of nation-states, free to create and express their own religious or ethnic identity or to disengage altogether from Jewish matters.

Within a period of fifty years, from 1880 to 1930, the Jewish population in the United States grew from an estimated 230,000 to 300,000 people to an estimated 4,228,000 to 4,400,000 people.[1] During the course of what came to be known as the Holocaust, one-third of world Jewry—approximately six million people—was systematically annihilated through an all-too-effective program of state-organized, industrialized murder. In 1948, the State of Israel was established in a portion of what had come to be known as Palestine. This followed a United Nations partition plan resolution in 1947 and the end of the British Mandate over the area. In short, there has been considerable change in the circumstances and settings of Jewish life in recent generations.

A Jew, today, can choose to identify as Jewish in any number of ways. Alternatively, a Jew can consciously or otherwise remain distant from anything distinctively Jewish. Moreover, for contemporary American Jews, Jewish identity is but one identity out of many. Such choices were not always available. Until recent centuries, a Jew generally had to join another faith community to sever ties with Jews and Judaism, and those who were part of the Jewish community were, in most times and places, expected to abide by fixed norms. As Jewish communal ties waned and Jewishness became, increasingly, a matter of choice, a literature developed through which authors shared their sense of the enduring value of Judaism and Jewish wisdom.

In 1836, Samson Raphael Hirsch, a rabbi serving the Jewish community in Oldenburg, in northwestern Germany, wrote a short book articulating a case for commitment to traditional Jewish thought and practice in the modern world. Known as *The Nineteen Letters*, Hirsch's work was framed as correspondence between a rabbi and a young intellectual who questioned Judaism's relevance to contemporary life. It attracted wide readership, leading to many further publications by the author, and was translated to English for American readers in 1899.[2]

In 1947, a prominent American rabbi, Milton Steinberg, authored *Basic Judaism*, aimed not only at "believing Jews" but at "that large body of heretofore indifferent Jews who, whether in response to pressures from without or voids within, are groping to establish rapport with the Jewish Tradition."[3]

This was followed, in 1959, by Herman Wouk's *This Is My God*.[4] Wouk, already an accomplished literary figure, set forth his personal understanding of Judaism and its enduring message; the book sold one hundred thousand copies within two months and was reprinted many times.

In 1975, two young American Jews, Dennis Prager and Joseph Telushkin, coauthored a book titled *Eight Questions People Ask about Judaism*.[5] They addressed Jews skeptical as to whether Jewish wisdom offered anything meaningful to Jews living in modern Western society. Two decades later, David Wolpe, a rabbi who had previously authored several books on aspects of Jewish thought, published a volume devoted to the question titled *Why Be Jewish?*[6] These books are but a sampling of a continuing literature—into the current decade—exploring the meaning that Judaism can hold for contemporary Jews and others interested in the wisdom expressed in its biblical and rabbinic texts.[7]

In the third decade of the twenty-first century, many Jews question or doubt the continuing relevance of Jewish texts and experiences to their lives. That said, over decades of teaching graduate and undergraduate students Jewish history at colleges and universities, and engaging with adult learners at Conservative, Orthodox, Reconstructionist, and Reform congregations, I have found that people's quest for meaning extends well beyond their interest in history. This book is designed for those embarked on such a search. It includes exploration of the content of the Torah and the themes central to each of its five books, as well as consideration of some of the implications and applications of those themes to the lives of twenty-first century readers.

This book does not focus on the history of the Torah or of events referenced in the Torah. Until recent centuries, Jews (as well as Christians) universally understood the Torah to have been divinely revealed at Mt. Sinai. Today, there are widely divergent views on the origins of this cornerstone text of Jewish self-understanding and instruction.[8]

Whether one views the Torah as divinely revealed—and there are multiple approaches to understanding the nature of revelation—or as an inspiring product of Jewish civilization, the Torah has influenced Jewish thought and action for millennia. Rabbi Jonathan Sacks comments that "no historical investigation will ever resolve the question of whether, at Sinai, the voice the Israelites heard was real or imagined."[9] Yet, he observes, "the story of the Jewish people, especially after the second Temple, is about one of the great love affairs of all time, the love of a people for a book, the Torah."[10]

The Torah has been interpreted and applied to life in varying times and places over the course of millennia. Certain of its laws, such as those relating to personal servitude, the stubborn and rebellious son, or the captive woman—each of which will be referenced in these pages—have, through an interpretive process, been regulated out of existence, over time. As we will see, this process continues, with interpreters invoking the very values articulated in the Torah as rationales for reinterpretation. The Torah remains a vital and instructive source of meaning for many who explore its teachings.

This volume draws upon commentaries authored over centuries that relate to diverse aspects of Torah teaching. It suggests that each of the five books of the Torah reflects a central theme: these are a connection to Israel, the Jews in history, ritual, community, and Jewish study. These themes, individually and collectively, can be sources of meaning for Jews living in the twenty-first century.

Five chapters of this volume are devoted to surveying the content of each book of the Torah with a focus on the primary theme(s) of those books. Each of these chapters is followed by exploration of that particular book's overarching theme and its contemporary applications; readers are encouraged to consider the meaning of these texts in their own life story. Though referencing many of the narratives and selected legal passages of the Torah, this survey is by no means exhaustive; it is intended as a starting point for further study.

Appropriating language from the Book of Proverbs (3:18), Jewish liturgy describes the Torah as "a tree of life to those who grasp her." Human perspectives are, however, diverse, and rabbinic tradition recognized that "there are seventy faces to the Torah" (Numbers Rabbah 13:15–16). The aim of this work is to share ideas, themes, values, and practices that are all part of a living Torah, with full awareness that personal meaning is, by definition, unique to each individual. "Living Torah" describes both Torah, as a vibrant text, and those who lead Torah-informed lives; "Torah informed" by no means implies uniformity of lifestyle.

In looking at the books that comprise the Torah—the first five books of the Hebrew Bible—a set of topic headings emerges. Genesis opens with prehistory: God, the world, and the role of humankind. Chapters 12 through 50 might be subtitled "the patriarchs and matriarchs of the Jewish people and their relationship to the land of Israel, with special attention to lessons from the lives of these early ancestors." The Book of Exodus turns to enslavement—following prosperity and abundant fertility—in Egypt; liberation, and the start of a journey to the land of Israel. It describes the making of a people with a distinctive past and vision of the future rooted in a sense of covenantal relationship. Leviticus, sometimes referred to as the Law of the Priests, is in large part a book of ritual, with considerable attention to "sanctification." Numbers relates to living in community, focusing on experiences of the tribes of Israel as they related to one another and as they encountered others, during decades of desert wandering. Deuteronomy, Moses's closing address to the Israelites, emphasizes education: the importance of learning and instructing successive generations in the teachings of Torah, the foundation of an enduring covenant. None of these themes is exclusive to a single book of the Torah; they are intertwined and developed throughout the Torah. Yet these headings are central motifs, and I have used them as thematic guides in these pages.

OF HISTORY, MEMORY, AND AN INTERPRETIVE TRADITION

Biblical Hebrew has no word for "history"; modern Hebrew has borrowed the word *historiah*. A recurring word, in the Hebrew Bible, however, is *zakhor*, memory/remembrance. Rabbi Jonathan Sacks points to a fundamental difference between history and memory. "History," he writes, "is an answer to the question 'What happened?' Memory is an answer to the question 'Who am I?' History is about facts; memory is about identity."[11]

Put otherwise, history is an attempt to reconstruct what happened; memory is about meaning-making. Remembrance in the Torah is presented as a collective imperative and is typically tied to a call to action. Thus, for example, memory of having been strangers and slaves in

Egypt is to inform the way Israelites treat the less fortunate in society (see, for example, Deuteronomy 24:17–18, 21–22).

The five books of the Torah are followed, immediately, in the Hebrew Bible by a series of books known as *nevi'im*, or prophets. Over the course of centuries, the prophets summoned the people Israel to adhere to the terms of the covenant. The closing exhortation, in the fifth century BCE, of the last of the prophets, Malachi, is: "Be mindful of the Teaching of My servant Moses, whom I charged at Horeb with laws and rules for all Israel" (Malachi 3:22). Mindfulness and application of the laws of the Torah, though, require interpretation and, in some cases, adjudication.

The Torah identifies the tribe of Levi as teachers of Torah (Deuteronomy 33:10) and indicates that when matters of legal judgment will arise, individuals are to "appear before the levitical priests, or the magistrate in charge at the time, and present your problem" (Deuteronomy 17:9). Ezra, an important teacher of Torah in the fifth century BCE, is described in the third section of the Hebrew Bible, *ketuvim*, or writings, as both a priest and a scribe (Ezra 7:1–6). However, over time, not all scribes or sages were priests (descendants of Moses's brother Aaron who was from the tribe of Levi) or Levites. Following the destruction of the Temple, in Jerusalem, 70 CE, the role and influence of the priests substantially declined, giving way, entirely, to expositors of Torah known as rabbis (literally, "teachers").

Sages or rabbis sometimes invoked oral tradition to explain the meaning of seemingly ambiguous passages of the Torah, describing those traditions as harking back to Moses. They also developed interpretive principles through which to arrive at an understanding of Torah law. Not only the Torah's legal passages but also its narratives were subjects of interpretation and commentary.

A dynamic, interpretive tradition ensured and continues to ensure that Torah speaks to the lives of readers in each generation, rendering it timeless—that is, not restricted to a particular time or place. Over the course of millennia, a literature surrounding the meaning, implications, and application of the Torah to contemporary life emerged. This book draws upon a broad selection of this literature in presenting the ideas explored.

Many who engage in Torah study speak of its interpreters in the present tense: "Rashi (1040–1105) says, Rambam (1135–1204) says,

Ramban (1194–1270) says." Each is in conversation with the other and with the contemporary student of Torah, across the generations. This book looks at the Torah narrative through the lens of classical and more contemporary Jewish commentators, encouraging the reader to join this continuing conversation. The meaning of Torah in the lives of its readers rather than its history accounts for its continuing impact.

Jonathan Sacks notes that Judaism "is about how a nation can be formed on the basis of shared commitment and collective responsibility. It is about how to construct a society that honors the human person as the image and likeness of God. It is about a vision, never fully realized but never abandoned, of a world based on justice and compassion."[12] Within this covenantal vision, the Torah speaks to each individual who engages with it, in a deeply personal way.

The Hebrew word for "heritage" (*morashah*) comes from the same root as the word "inheritance" (*yerushah*). No less than an inheritance, one's heritage is surely worthy of exploration. In each Torah scroll, there are, typically, four blank lines setting apart one book of the Torah from the next. This open area separating the books can, perhaps, be understood as leaving space for the unique ways in which each individual who engages in Torah study integrates and applies the themes of the five books to their own life. It is my hope that this slender volume will contribute to each reader's appreciation of the "heritage of the congregation of Jacob," as the Torah is described toward its close (Deuteronomy 33:4).

Chapter 1

The Book of Genesis

Humankind and the World; The Land of Israel in Jewish Memory

GOD, THE WORLD, AND HUMANKIND
(CHAPTERS 1 THROUGH 11)

It has long been customary for Jews to read chapters of the Torah each week as part of an annual cycle of study and synagogue ritual. On the holiday of Simḥat Torah, literally "rejoicing in Torah," Jews throughout the world complete the Torah cycle and begin it afresh. The Torah is divided into fifty-four portions; during some weeks, there is a double portion, to ensure that the cycle reaches its close on Simḥat Torah. Remarkably, there are but two Torah portions that relate to God, the world, and humankind prior to the introduction of Abraham and Sarah, the patriarch and matriarch of the Jewish people. These two Torah portions span chapters 1 through 11 in the Book of Genesis, known in Hebrew by the opening word of the book, *B'reishit* (literally, in the beginning).

Genesis opens with the creation of heaven and earth. God's existence is neither demonstrated nor discussed; it is an underlying premise: "When God began to create heaven and earth" (Genesis 1:1). The declaration expresses belief in a Power beyond the capacity of humankind to fully comprehend. The creation narrative likewise assumes that the Creator God takes an abiding interest in the world and, particularly, in humankind.

In a sentence taken from Isaiah (6:3)—of whose words, among the biblical prophets, the most are extant—Jewish liturgy pronounces: "*kadosh, kadosh, kadosh* The Lord of Hosts! His presence fills all the earth!" The word *kadosh* is commonly translated as holy. The Hebrew word, however, means separate, distinctive, set apart: other. God cannot be fully understood; God's ways are not altogether fathomable. In Isaiah's words: "For My plans are not your plans, Nor are My ways your ways—declares the Lord" (55:8). The great medieval Jewish philosopher and legal scholar Maimonides (1135–1204) asks what Moses, whom the Torah identifies as the greatest of the prophets (Deuteronomy 34:10), wanted to see when he asked God: "Oh, let me behold Your Presence!" (Exodus 33:18). Maimonides explains: "He desired to know the truth of the existence of the Holy One, blessed is He. . . . And He, blessed is He, answered him, that it is not within the intellectual power of the living person, who is a composite of body and soul, to reach the pure truth of this matter" (*Mishneh Torah*, Foundations of the Torah, 1:10). Belief in God is forever a matter of faith rather than of certainty by demonstrable knowledge. "Faith," writes Jonathan Sacks, "is not certainty. It is the courage to live with uncertainty. It is not knowing all the answers. It is often the strength to live with the questions."[1]

One of the names of God, in Jewish tradition, is *Ha-Makom*; literally, "the place." A rabbinic text of the sixth century explains that God is the place of the world, and the world is not God's place (Genesis Rabbah 68:5). God is not restricted to any location, the Torah teaches; the name *Ha-Makom* expresses God's pervasiveness throughout the universe.

Each person understands God in their unique way. "Wonder, or radical amazement," writes Abraham Joshua Heschel, "is our honest response to the grandeur and mystery of reality."[2] In a prayer recited by many Jews three times each day, traditional Jewish liturgy references "the God of Abraham; the God of Isaac; the God of Jacob." Though each of these ancestors of the Jewish people recognized one God in the world with whom they stood in covenantal relationship, they each related to God in their unique ways, as have individuals throughout Jewish history.

The Torah lays no claim to scientific truth and, as Rabbi Sacks notes, "no unified field theory will ever finally settle the question of whether or not the universe was created by a personal God."[3] Science and religion explore different domains. While the scientist discovers facts and learns more about the laws of nature, religion deals with such questions as the purpose of life and how best to live in this world. Human beings did not create the natural order, but we are creators of the societies in which we live. My father, an accomplished physicist with tremendous curiosity about the world, is at the same time a devoted student of Torah; the two realms are complementary, not competing, dimensions of human interest.

From its opening verses, the Torah communicates that there is one ultimate Power in the universe; there are not multiple gods or competing forces of light and darkness. The one God is entirely unique and limitless. Humankind, we read, is fashioned in the Divine image (Genesis 1:26), endowed with understanding and intellect and possessed of free will.

The Mishnah, a collection of oral teachings compiled more than 1,800 years ago, notes that humankind began from a single ancestor so that no one should declare "my father is greater than your father." The idea that all of humankind begins with one couple teaches that saving a single life is as though preserving a whole universe (Sanhedrin 4:5). The dignity of each individual is not, necessarily, a "self-evident" truth, as demonstrated throughout human history; it is, however, a foundational principle of the Torah.

In approaching the narratives of Genesis, Nahum Sarna, in his book *Understanding Genesis*, comments that literalism can diminish from understanding and appreciating the meaning and enduring relevance of the Torah's narratives.[4] Throughout the ages, interpreters of the Hebrew Bible have focused on lessons to be learned from these texts. Sarna draws attention to the optimism associated with the creation narrative and the profound sense of human potential that it conveys.

People, the Torah teaches, are free moral agents and bear responsibility for their actions. Initially given but one instruction—not to eat the fruit of a particular tree—woman and man share the fruit of that tree. Each bears responsibility and is, accordingly, punished.

Among their progeny, Cain slays his brother Abel. "Where is your brother Abel?" God asks (Genesis 4:9). Famously, Cain replies with words commonly translated, "Am I my brother's keeper?"

The Torah text does not include punctuation, leaving considerable room for multiple readings of a given verse. In Hebrew, Cain's response reads: *Ha-shomer aḥi anokhi*. The word *anokhi*, I, is also used in the Torah as a reference to God (as, for example, "I [*Anokhi*] the Lord am your God") (Exodus 20:2). The *Midrash Tanḥuma*, a collection of rabbinic interpretations dating back more than a millennium, suggests that Cain is declaring: You, God (*Anokhi*) are my brother's keeper. By holding Cain accountable, God affirms that it is Cain who bears responsibility for his own actions. Moreover, "the bloods of your brother cry out to me." Not only has Cain murdered Abel but any potential descendants have been annihilated.

The biblical narrative relates that, over the course of generations, wickedness became increasingly pervasive. Granted free will but no guidance, humankind makes poor choices. It is at this point that the Torah introduces Noah, described as a righteous person in his generation (Genesis 6:9), and tells of a devastating flood that destroys all but Noah and his family and the animals sheltered on the ark that he had built at God's instruction.

After the flood, a covenant is pronounced. God promises that never again will God cause a catastrophic flood cutting off all flesh; the sign of that covenant is a rainbow (Genesis 9:13). The covenant is universal, "between Me and all flesh that is on the earth" (Genesis 9:17).

Noah's children, the Talmud (a later compilation of Jewish law) explains, are commanded (1) to establish laws, (2) not to curse God, (3) not to practice idolatry, (4) not to engage in illicit sexual activity, (5) not to shed the blood of humans, (6) not to steal, and (7) not to eat the limb of a living animal (Sanhedrin 56a). Humankind is to flourish and teem on the earth (Genesis 9:7). All humankind, Judaism teaches, is bound by the Noahide laws, as part of a postdiluvial, covenantal relationship.

In the ensuing generations, the course of human conduct again proves disappointing. Chapter 11 of Genesis opens with a narrative of the Tower of Babel. It is a story in which uniformity leads to the anonymity of individuals and a devaluation of human life. It is also a condemnation of the social ills that can emerge from urban life.

Pirkei de-Rabbi Eliezer, a collection of rabbinic teachings compiled 1,200 years ago, recounts that, as the homogeneous human collective settled in one spot and undertook construction of a great tower, there was no regard for an individual builder who might plummet from the heights to his death. When, however, a brick would fall and break, they would "sit and cry and lament: 'When will we have another one to replace it?'" (*Pirkei de-Rabbi Eliezer*, 24). The eradication of human uniqueness was an assault on the dignity of humankind; the corrective was that "the Lord scattered them from there over the face of the whole earth" (Genesis 11:8). Diversity rather than uniformity, the Book of Genesis suggests, helps maintain human dignity.

In the course of its opening eleven chapters, the Torah describes a world created by a Divine Power with an abiding hope that humankind will build societies reflecting the Divine image inherent in each individual. Ten generations pass from Adam and Eve to Noah and his family, a further ten generations from Noah to Abraham. Human potential has yet to be realized. As, at the close of the Torah's first "installment" in the weekly cycle of Torah study, the reader is introduced to Noah, the second Torah portion closes with an introduction to Abraham (known, initially, as Abram), who represents a new phase in covenantal relationship between God and humankind.

GENESIS 12–50: LESSONS FROM THE LIVES OF THE PATRIARCHS AND MATRIARCHS; THE ISRAEL CONNECTION

Chapter 12 of Genesis opens with God instructing Abram (later renamed Abraham) to go to the land that God will show him. There he will become a great nation and a blessing to others. Rashi (1040–1105), the great medieval Jewish commentator on the Torah, poses the following question at the very start of Genesis: Because the Torah is largely a body of law, why does it not begin with Exodus 12 and the opening commandment (there) directed to the Jewish people?

The answer, suggests Rashi—writing nearly a millennium ago—is that the nations of the world will, one day, ask: By what right do the Jews lay claim to the land of Israel? The Book of Genesis opens, Rashi notes, with God's creating the world and leads to a covenant between God and Abraham and his descendants. That covenant includes an enduring tie to the land that God shows Abraham in Genesis 12 and that the patriarchs and matriarchs inhabited and traversed.

The narratives of Genesis 12–50 associate the land of Israel with the very origins of the Jewish people. A Divine promise that the land of Israel will be granted to them and their descendants is made successively to Abraham, Isaac, and Jacob. The patriarchs pitch their tents in various parts of the land; they interact with local inhabitants, dig wells, build altars, assign names to numerous places, and most are buried in an area purchased by Abraham as the final resting place of the matriarch Sarah (Rachel, we read, dies after giving birth to her second son, Benjamin, and is buried on the road, near Bethlehem [Genesis 35:19]).

Jacob, who dies in Egypt, asks to be buried in his family's ancestral burial cave. Joseph, who lived most of his life in Egypt and was buried there, asks his surviving family to reinter him when, one day, they will collectively return to the land of Israel. The "Israel connection" extends even through those chapters near the close of Genesis in which the entire family of Jacob—the children of Israel—resides outside the land.

Another aspect of the narratives of Genesis 12–50 is the lessons they hold for later generations. Ramban, also known as Nahmanides (1194–1270), notes that occurrences in the lives of Israel's ancestors serve as signs or guides for future generations. Alongside the Israel connection stands the didactic value of studying the lives of the people—Israel's early ancestors—as presented in the Torah.

PARTICULARISM AND UNIVERSALISM

Genesis 12:2 includes both a promise to Abram that "I will make of you a great nation" and an indication that "you shall be a blessing." On Abram's arrival in Canaan, "the land I will show you" (Genesis 12:1), God appears to him and says: "I will assign this land to your offspring" (Genesis 12:7). The seminomadic patriarchs and matriarchs dwell in various parts of the land of Israel, digging wells, building altars, and relating to various individuals and groups of people in their environment. Abraham is to serve as an example to others, as well as his descendants. Though party to a particular covenant, Abraham was to be a blessing to all of humanity.

Abram's change of name to Abraham is noted in Genesis 17:5 as he is told that he will be the father of many nations (*ha* representing the Hebrew word *hamon*, meaning many; Abraham will become the "father of a multitude of nations"). Again, God promises: "I assign the land you sojourn in to you and your offspring to come, all the land of Canaan, as an everlasting holding" (17:8); circumcision is to serve as a sign of this covenant (Genesis 17:10–14). Sarah, formerly known as Sarai, is included in the covenantal promise: "I will bless her; indeed, I will give you a son by her. I will bless her so that she shall give rise to nations; rulers of peoples shall issue from her" (Genesis 17:16).

Ten generations after the covenant with Noah and his descendants, the Torah presents a more particular covenant between God and Abraham and his descendants, but that covenant is to have universal impact. Right conduct is integral to the covenantal relationship. God says of Abraham: "For I have singled him out, that he may instruct his children and his posterity to keep the way of the Lord by doing what is just and right (*tzedakah u'mishpat*)" (Genesis 18:19).

The term *tzedakah* comes from the Hebrew word *tzedek*, meaning justice. As a contemporary scholar of Jewish law explains, "The Torah's vision of justice includes both procedural and substantive elements. That is, it demands in court that we ensure fairness by following specific procedures in judging people ('procedural justice') and in society generally we must guarantee that there is a substantial safety net so that the poor, orphans, and widows get what they need to live, receive an education, and find a mate ('substantive justice')."[5] *Mishpat* comes from the word *shofet*, judge, and refers to judgments and rules. Commitment to actions that are just and right can sometimes mean acting in ways that are different. A midrash suggests that Abraham was called *ha'ivri*, "the Hebrew," because "all the world was on one side (*be'ever eḥad*) and he was on the other" (Genesis Rabbah 42:8).

THE LAND AND COVENANTAL SOCIETY

Early on (Genesis 15:13), God tells Abram that his offspring will spend hundreds of years as aliens in a land not their own. There they will be oppressed; they will, however, leave with great wealth (15:14). The enslavement of the Israelites in Egypt is thus foretold.

The land that Abraham's descendants will possess is, in his lifetime, home to no fewer than ten peoples (Genesis 15:19–21). The laws of the Torah, detailed in the books following Genesis, include many

instructions relating to life and society in the land of Israel. Full implementation of covenantal obligations and responsibilities would await
the return of Abraham's descendants to the land of Israel following an
extended period outside the land.

OF KINDNESS AND ACTIVISM

Chapter 18 of Genesis opens with Abraham sitting at the entrance of his
tent, in the heat of the day. Seeing three men—complete strangers—he
runs to greet them, welcomes them, provides water, and asks his wife,
Sarah, to prepare a sumptuous meal. After sharing with Abraham the
news that, in the year ahead, Sarah will bear a son, the visitors proceed
in the direction of Sodom.

At that point, God discloses to Abraham that the outcry of people in
Sodom and Gomorrah is so great that God plans to destroy those cities.
Abraham remonstrates with God: "Shall not the Judge of all the earth
deal justly?" (Genesis 18:25). Supposing that there is surely a critical
mass—even as few as ten—of righteous people in Sodom, "within
the city," Abraham confronts God with the proposition that it would
be unjust to destroy the entire community, "the innocent as well as
the guilty."

Abraham, an activist, recognizes the importance of involvement
"within the city" (Genesis 18:24). Even before negotiating on behalf
of Sodom, he liberated his nephew, Lot, when he was taken captive
in a regional conflict (14:12–16). To have impact, righteous people
need to be active in the public square. Though God agrees to spare the
city should there be ten righteous people, such a population does not
exist in Sodom.

ISHMAEL AND ISAAC

Childless for decades, Sarah brings her Egyptian maidservant, Hagar,
to her husband, saying, "Look, the Lord has kept me from bearing.
Consort with my maid; perhaps I shall have a son through her" (Genesis
16:2). Drawing upon texts of Near Eastern cultures, Nahum Sarna notes

that "the custom of an infertile wife providing her husband with a concubine is well documented."[6]

The union of Abraham and Hagar results in the birth of a son, Ishmael. When, later, Sarah—as presaged by Abraham's visitors—bears a son, Isaac, there is discord in the household. Although Hagar and Ishmael are eventually banished, Ishmael is clearly identified as a son of Abraham; the Torah later relates that Abraham's "sons Isaac and Ishmael buried him in the cave of Machpelah" (Genesis 25:9). Distraught at the time of their banishment, Hagar is assured that God will make a great nation of Ishmael (Genesis 21:18).

Among the most difficult passages of the Torah for contemporary readers is the "binding of Isaac," described in Genesis 22. The promise of a child to Sarah is fulfilled, and the child, Isaac, is circumcised per the instruction of Genesis 17:12, on the eighth day. Sometime later, Abraham hears and obeys God's call to take his beloved son Isaac and bind him as a sacrifice. Though, eventually, Abraham is told to desist from sacrificing his son, the story is troubling; all the more so, as Abraham is praised "because you have obeyed My command" (Genesis 22:18).

Commentators throughout the ages have struggled with this episode. Child sacrifice is something from which the modern reader recoils. The same Abraham who did not hesitate to take issue with God's readiness to destroy Sodom and Gomorrah proceeds without question to act on God's instruction to bind his son as a sacrifice.

Twenty-first-century scholar Ethan Tucker, observes: "Abraham would never have agreed to murder his son, just as he was horrified that God was set to murder the innocent people of S'dom. But human sacrifice was not murder to him, even as it seems so to us."[7] Tucker suggests that contemporary readers are summoned to give of ourselves in pursuit of worthy ends, as Abraham was prepared to do in his time within the context of his understanding of God and religious expression. The Torah dramatically calls attention to the instruction to desist from human sacrifice. Describing a God of mercy, compassion, and justice, the Torah calls for pursuit of *kedushah*, sanctification, by dedicating oneself to God's ways.

CARRYING FORWARD A LEGACY

Immediately following the death of Sarah, Abraham purchases a burial place for his wife (Genesis 23:4–18). This is Abraham's first real estate acquisition in the Promised Land. Abraham next turns to finding a wife for his son, Isaac, heir to the Divine promise; he instructs his servant to go to his kindred in Haran for this purpose.

Abraham's servant embarks on this journey. Arriving at a well in the environs of Haran at evening time, the servant prays to the God of Abraham: "Let the maiden to whom I say, 'Please lower your jug that I may drink,' and who replies, 'Drink, and I will also water your camels'—let her be the one whom You have decreed for Your servant Isaac" (Genesis 24:14). Recognizing the value of kindness in the household of Abraham, the servant intuits that such a test will yield a prospective spouse whose ethos are aligned with those of the family.

Scarcely does he finish his prayer than the servant encounters Rebecca. She conducts herself just as the servant had prayed; he inquires about her family and learns that Rebecca is Abraham's kin. Proceeding to her family's home, the servant tells of his mission, his prayer, and Rebecca's actions at the well. Rebecca, of her own accord, and with the blessing of her family, agrees to return with the servant to Canaan, there to become Isaac's wife.

The Torah relates that Abraham took another wife named Keturah (Genesis 25:1) and that he had six sons by her. To those children, he gave gifts and sent them to the land of the east (Genesis 25:6). On Abraham's death, he is buried by Isaac and Ishmael. After listing the descendants of Ishmael and noting the passing of Ishmael, the Torah turns to the continuing narrative of the patriarchs and matriarchs of the Jewish people, starting with Isaac and Rebecca.

ISAAC AND REBECCA AND THEIR SONS

Though childless for some time, Rebecca eventually conceives and is pregnant with twins; "the children struggled in her womb" (Genesis 25:22). The struggle, God tells her, presages sibling rivalry, albeit the outcome is predestined: "Two nations are in your womb, Two separate peoples shall issue from your body; One people shall be mightier than the other, And the older shall serve the younger" (Genesis 25:23). Esau is the first born; Jacob, his twin, grasps his brother's heel (hence the name Jacob, from the Hebrew word "heel") during childbirth.

As the brothers grew, Esau was a man of the field, a skilled hunter; Jacob was a mild man, who stayed in the tents. Esau was favored by Isaac; Jacob by Rebecca. There is no indication that Rebecca at any point shared with Isaac her intimation that Jacob was to be the bearer of the covenant of Abraham. The reader of the narrative cannot but wonder at the (better) possible outcomes that might have emerged were there to have been communication between Rebecca and Isaac.

Though identified prenatally as the one who would be ascendant, Jacob engages in two acts of acquiring the birthright from his first-born twin brother. First, Esau returns from the field, famished, as Jacob is cooking a stew. Jacob responds to Esau's request for food by insisting that he sell the birthright in exchange. Only when Esau swears to such a sale does Jacob give his brother food and drink (Genesis 25:30–34). Later, when Isaac instructs Esau to hunt and prepare him food, whereupon he will bless him—a conversation overheard by Rebecca—Jacob agrees to and executes his mother's directive to impersonate Esau to receive his blind father's blessing (Genesis 27:6–29).

Nahum Sarna observes that, while the Torah relates that Abraham died at "a good ripe age, old and contented" (Genesis 25:8) and Isaac is described as dying "in ripe old age" (Genesis 35:29), the aging Jacob—asked about the years of his life by a welcoming Egyptian Pharaoh—replies that the years of his sojourn have been "few and hard" (Genesis 47:9). Sarna comments that "the biographical details of Jacob's life read like a catalogue of misfortunes," reflecting "condemnation of Jacob's moral lapse in his treatment of his brother and father."[8] The Torah and later books of the Bible do not refrain from detailing the moral failings of Scriptures' most eminent personalities; these, too, are instructive.

Recognizing the intense fury of Esau who returns from the hunt and learns of his brother's deception, Rebecca, with Isaac's agreement, encourages Jacob to go to Haran in search of a wife. Rebecca will not again see her beloved son, Jacob. Jacob spends twenty years in the employ of his uncle, Laban. As he deceived Isaac, Jacob is, in turn, deceived by Laban, who substitutes his daughter Leah for the promised Rachel, for whose hand in marriage Jacob had toiled seven years (Genesis 29:20–25).

During his years in Haran, Jacob fathers eleven sons and a daughter by his wives Leah and Rachel and their maidservants Zilpah and Bilhah. Jacob and his family, and the considerable flocks of sheep that Jacob earned in the course of his work for Laban, eventually leave Haran and head toward Canaan. It is interesting to compare the dreams of Jacob on setting out to Haran and as he decides to leave Haran.

On leaving his parental home toward Haran, Jacob stops for the night. In a dream, he sees a ladder connecting heaven and earth, with angels ascending and descending. He perceives God assuring him that the ground on which he is lying will be assigned to his offspring and that his descendants will be as the dust of the earth; moreover, God will protect him and bring him back to the land (Genesis 28:12–15). After twenty years in Haran, Jacob reports to his wives that he has dreamed of streaked and speckled goats, a dream no doubt precipitated by his arrangements with Laban as to which animals belonged to Laban and which to him. It is in the course of that dream that God summons Jacob to return to his native land; it is time to move on (Genesis 31:10–13).

After parting from Laban with his family and flocks, Jacob learns that his brother Esau is approaching with four hundred men. Jacob's entourage crosses the Jabbok River; Jacob is left alone as he awaits the encounter with Esau. During the night, an unknown assailant wrestles with Jacob, until the break of dawn (Genesis 32:25). Though the assailant injures Jacob, wrenching his hip at its socket, the attacker cannot prevail. Jacob refuses to release him until exacting a blessing. That blessing is the bestowal of a new name, Israel, "for you have striven with beings divine and human, and have prevailed" (Genesis 32:29). The "children of Israel" have, over millennia, encountered struggles of a variety of sorts but have endured and thrived.

Jacob and Esau are, ostensibly, reconciled, and they together bury their father Isaac, when he dies "in ripe old age" (Genesis 35:29). Jacob experiences a series of troubles in Canaan: his only daughter, Dinah, is violated (Genesis 34:2), his beloved wife Rachel dies soon after childbirth (Genesis 35:16–20), and Rachel's first-born son, Joseph, is— unbeknownst to Jacob—kidnapped by his brothers and sold into slavery (Genesis 37:27–28). The account of Joseph and his brothers occupies much of Genesis 37–50; this extended narrative is the closing phase in the formative saga of ancient Israel.

JOSEPH: FROM PAMPERED SON, TO SLAVE, TO EGYPTIAN VICEROY

The Joseph story opens with estrangement between Joseph and his brothers. Joseph is Israel's most beloved son. Jacob (Israel) makes him an ornamental tunic; "and when his brothers saw that their father loved him more than any of his brothers, they hated him so that they could not speak a friendly word to him" (Genesis 37:4). Joseph's conduct does nothing to endear him to his brothers. Not only does he bring bad reports of his brothers to his father, he shares with his family dreams in which his brothers' sheaves bow down to his sheaf and in which the sun, the moon and eleven stars bow to him.

Sent by his father to see how his brothers, pasturing the flock in Shekhem, are faring, Joseph sets out to join them. As the dreamer approaches, the brothers seize him, strip him of his tunic, and throw him into a pit (Genesis 37:23–24). Seeing some passing merchants, Judah suggests selling him as a slave, and the brothers act on that plan. Joseph is transported to Egypt and sold to Potiphar, a courtier of Pharaoh (Genesis 37:36). The brothers, meanwhile, dip Joseph's tunic in the blood of a kid and take it to Jacob; Jacob concludes that Joseph was torn by a wild animal and refuses to be comforted (Genesis 37:33–35).

The text digresses to relate an episode in the life of Judah. Judah and his wife had three sons. The first-born, we read, married a woman named Tamar. That son died and, as he was childless, Tamar's brother-in-law was obligated by prevailing norms to take the widow of his brother as his wife to provide an heir for him. When the second son died soon thereafter, Judah withheld his remaining son, Shelah, instructing Tamar: "Stay as a widow in your father's house until my son Shelah grows up" (Genesis 38:11).

Over the course of time, Judah's wife dies and, independent of that, Tamar sees that though Shelah has grown, there is no movement toward a relationship with Tamar. Learning that Judah is heading to Timnah for sheep shearing, she takes off her widow's garb, covers her face with a veil, and stands by the roadside. Taking her for a prostitute, Judah sleeps with his daughter-in-law. She exacts from him his seal, cord, and staff—valuable personal items—as a pledge against a kid from the flock that he promises by way of payment.

Though Judah sends someone to find the prostitute by the road to make good on his pledge, the local townspeople indicate that there is no prostitute at that location. Subsequently, Judah learns that his widowed daughter-in-law is pregnant. His immediate reaction is that she should be burned. She quietly sends him the seal, cord, and staff he had left with her, indicating that "I am with child by the man to whom these belong" (Genesis 38:25). Judah recognizes the items and says: "she is more in the right than I, inasmuch as I did not give her to my son Shelah" (Genesis 38:26). When a woman, Tamar, acts in a bold and assertive manner to correct an injustice, God approves; she is rewarded with inclusion in the line of David.

King David's ancestry traces to a child of the cohabitation of Judah and Tamar. An important dimension of leadership—and a quality that will be manifested by King David—is acknowledging error. This episode is the first of several demonstrating growing maturity on the part of Judah, Leah's fourth-born son.

It is worthy of note that the name Judah, which comes to be the name of the land and Kingdom of Judah, later known as Judea, and, hence, the origin of the appellation Jew, comes from an expression of gratitude. When Leah gave birth to her fourth son she declared: "'This time I will praise the Lord.' Therefore, she named him Judah" (Genesis 29:35). That name, which comes from a Hebrew root meaning "to praise," bespeaks appreciation and thanksgiving; gratitude is embedded in the very name by which Jews are known.

Joseph, to whom the narrative returns, matures, as does Judah, over time. Potiphar, Joseph's master, takes a liking to him and places him in charge of his household. Joseph refuses the advances of Potiphar's wife, both because it would violate the trust accorded him by his master and because it would be a sin against God (Genesis 39:9). Finally, Potiphar's wife seizes his garment; as Joseph flees, she screams and claims that Joseph tried to force himself on her. Notably, she points to the *ivri*, the Hebrew man—the "other"—that Potiphar had brought to the household, appealing to the prejudices and jealousies of fellow Egyptians (Genesis 39:14).

Joseph is incarcerated and gains the favor of the jailer, who places the prisoners in Joseph's charge. Among the prisoners are the cupbearer and the baker of Pharoah. Each has a dream; and, in each case, Joseph interprets the dream. In the case of the cupbearer, Joseph foretells that he will be restored to his position; in the case of the baker, he interprets the dream to mean that the baker will be executed. In each case, Joseph predicts that the event he foresees will take place three days hence. On the third day, the events Joseph foretold are actualized.

Two years after the cupbearer's release from jail and return to the service of Pharaoh, Pharaoh has troubling dreams that no one can interpret. The cupbearer recounts to Pharaoh that, at a time when he and the baker were in custody, there was a Hebrew youth with them who interpreted the meaning of each man's dream. As he interpreted, so did things come to pass (Genesis 41:9–13).

Pharaoh sends for Joseph. When he appears, Pharaoh tells him that he has heard that he can tell the meaning of dreams. Joseph replies: "Not I! God will see to Pharaoh's welfare" (41:16). The haughty lad of chapter 37 has, by chapter 41, developed a measure of humility.

Joseph interprets Pharaoh's dreams as foreshadowing seven years of plenty to be followed by seven difficult years and suggests that Pharaoh take steps to store food during the good years to prepare reserves for the years that will follow. Joseph, now thirty years of age, is placed in a position of responsibility, second only to Pharaoh, to oversee this project. Joseph is married to Asenath, daughter of Poti-phera, priest of On, and fathers two sons, Manasseh and Ephraim.

THE CHILDREN OF ISRAEL REUNITED IN EGYPT

As Joseph foresaw, there were seven years of plenty, followed by famine, throughout the area. Because Egypt had stockpiles of grain, people came to purchase food from its granaries. Ten of Joseph's brothers—all but Benjamin, Jacob's second son by his beloved Rachel—come to Egypt to buy provender. Though they do not recognize Joseph, he immediately recognizes them. He sends them to Canaan with food but creates a situation where, if they are to return for further provisions, they must bring Benjamin.

When, eventually, they return with Benjamin, Joseph places the brothers in a desperate situation—accusing Benjamin of stealing his divining goblet—which will test whether his brothers have remorse for their earlier actions and will act accordingly. Judah, who had proposed the sale of Joseph decades earlier, steps forward and implores Pharaoh's viceroy to keep him as a servant and send Benjamin back to his aged father with his brothers: "For how can I go back to my father unless the boy is with me? Let me not be witness to the woe that would overtake my father!" (Genesis 44:34).

Joseph discloses his identity to his brothers, adding: "Now, do not be distressed or reproach yourselves because you sold me hither; it was to save life that God sent me ahead of you" (Genesis 45:5). Pharaoh invites the extended family of Joseph to come settle in the land of Egypt: "And never mind your belongings, for the best of all the land of Egypt shall be yours" (Genesis 45:20). Jacob, told by his sons that Joseph is alive and that he is viceroy of Egypt, has a vision in which God tells him: "Fear not to go down to Egypt, for I will make you there into a great nation. I Myself will go down with you to Egypt, and I Myself will also bring you back; and Joseph's hand shall close your eyes" (Genesis 46:3–4).

Jacob, with his children and grandchildren, travels to Egypt, at the invitation of Pharaoh. The Torah relates that Jacob "sent Judah ahead of him to Joseph *le-horot le-fanav Goshna*" (Genesis 46:28). The verse is commonly translated "to point the way before him to Goshen." Rashi offers this as the plain meaning of the text but adds, quoting earlier rabbinic sources, that the word *le-horot*, meaning to teach, can imply that Jacob sent Judah ahead to establish a house of study, a reflection of the longstanding commitment of Jewish communities to ensuring educational opportunity for successive generations.

Toward the end of his life, Jacob blesses Ephraim and Manasseh; they will be counted among the landed tribes of Israel. Moreover, "By you (Ephraim and Manasseh) shall Israel invoke blessings, saying: God make you like Ephraim and Manasseh" (Genesis 48:20). Jacob speaks to his sons: "he bade them farewell, addressing to each a parting word appropriate to him" (Genesis 49:28). That each is distinctive, the verse suggests, serves as a source of blessing to the collective.

Sensing that his death is near, Jacob, who lived in Egypt seventeen years, instructs his sons to bury him in the cave in the field of Machpelah, in Canaan, that Abraham had purchased from the Hittites. The brothers carry out their father's wishes. Fearing that Joseph might yet bear a grudge for the wrong they had long ago perpetrated, the brothers tell Joseph that Jacob had asked that he forgive their wrongdoing; they are, they say, prepared to be his slaves. Joseph assures them that they need not fear: "although you intended me harm, God intended it for good, so as to bring about the present result—the survival of many people" (Genesis 50:20).

Genesis closes with the death of Joseph. As his death nears, Joseph says to his brothers: "'I am about to die. God will surely take notice of you and bring you up from this land to the land that He promised on oath to Abraham, to Isaac, and to Jacob.' So Joseph made the sons of Israel swear, saying: 'When God has taken notice of you, you shall carry up my bones from here'" (Genesis 50:24–25).

The theme of connection between the people Israel and the land of Israel, introduced in Genesis 12, extends to the closing chapter of the first book of the Torah; it will frequently reappear in the books that follow. Joseph dies and is buried in Egypt. With his passing, the formative period of ancient Israel reaches its close. The stage is set for the nation-building, covenantal narrative that is to follow.

Chapter 2

God, Israel, and the Jews' Ongoing Conversation

When today many Jews profess that they are Jewish albeit of no religion, they are typically affirming either or both of the following: (a) I don't believe in God—or at least not in a notion of God that I associate with Judaism; (b) I have little or no use for institutionalized religion. For Jewish "nones" (that is, of no religion), the themes of the Torah can—as for Jews who affirm a religious orientation—be highly instructive. Micah Goodman points out that "Judaism is the Jews' ongoing conversation." He observes that "one precondition for joining any conversation is a basic familiarity with its context. If we want to engage in a political debate, we must be familiar with the political context; and if we want to engage in a scientific debate, we must understand something about the science. And in order to join the intergenerational conversation about Judaism, Jews need to be familiar with its contents."[1] It is on that backdrop that five chapters of this book are devoted to a basic overview of the Torah, the foundational text of the ongoing, intergenerational conversation that is Judaism.

In his book *How to Read the Bible*, Bible scholar Marc Brettler notes that the Bible includes multiple opinions on a variety of matters, among them the nature of God. As a Jew who takes the Bible seriously in his religious life, Brettler—within his community—transforms the Bible from sourcebook (a collection of sometimes diverse perspectives) to textbook (an instructive guidebook) "by selecting, revaluing, and interpreting the texts that I call sacred."[2] This, he suggests, is not unlike the approach of classical commentaries that have interpreted the Bible throughout the centuries. The book you are reading, similarly, reflects choices from the Torah text and its many interpretations; this is part of the intergenerational conversation that is Judaism.

After presenting God as creator of heaven and earth, manifesting will and consciousness, and as an abiding Presence, with interest in humankind, Genesis is largely devoted to the association of the Jewish people's forebearers with the land of Israel. The Torah introduces God as both powerful and good. As the text unfolds, the people Israel is called to relate to God with a combination of awe and love and to actualize such Godly attributes as kindness and compassion. Yet as Micah Goodman aptly notes, "Jewish thinkers have never agreed about who or what God is."[3] Whether to conceive of God as transcendent (existing apart from and not subject to the limitations of the material universe) or immanent (pervading and operating within the universe) or whether one can better apprehend God through reason or experience, are matters about which Jews have differed throughout the ages. While affirming God, Jews have held varying notions of both God and revelation.

In the nineteenth century, a variety of streams of Jewish thought developed in response to the encounter of Jews and Judaism with modernity. Among these new "movements" in Jewish thought were Reform, Orthodox, and Conservative (earlier known as Positive Historical) Judaism. Each of these approaches has evolved during the ensuing centuries; each recognizes the limits of human theological understanding. So, for example, Emanuel Rackman—a late twentieth-century modern Orthodox rabbi and scholar—observed: "It may be intellectually challenging, even exciting, to philosophize and theologize, but let us reconcile ourselves to the one inescapable truth: God is beyond understanding."[4] The Reform movement's 1999 Statement of Principles pronounces: "We affirm the reality and oneness of God, even as we may differ in our understanding of the Divine Presence."[5] Writing at mid-twentieth century, (Conservative) Rabbi Milton Steinberg declared: "Affirming God, Judaism permits considerable latitude as to conceptions of Him."[6]

Neither Steinberg's use of the male pronoun nor its use in this volume is to suggest that God is of a particular gender. Though masculine references to God are prevalent, Jewish mysticism heavily invokes female imagery in its vocabulary about God. Tamar Ross writes: "It (kabbalah) not only uses female metaphors for the *shekhinah* aspect of God, but also images of God birthing, nursing, and nurturing the world after protecting its initial emanation in the womb of *Binah*, the higher mother."[7]

As earlier noted, religious seekers—including Moses himself—can, the Torah communicates, never behold God but only arrive at a sense of God's Presence. Humankind can and should, the Torah emphasizes, focus on Godly conduct. As the Talmud frames it:

> Rabbi Hama, son of Rabbi Hanina, said: "What is the meaning of the verse, 'Follow none but the Lord your God, and revere none but Him; observe His commandments alone, and heed only His orders; worship none but Him, and hold fast to Him' (Deut. 13:5)? . . . A person should imitate the righteous ways of the Holy One, blessed be He. Just as the Lord clothed the naked, . . . so too you must supply clothes for the naked. Just as the Holy One, blessed be He, visited the sick, . . . so too you should visit the sick. Just as the Holy One, blessed be He, buried the dead, . . . so too you must bury the dead. Just as the Holy One, blessed be He, comforted mourners, . . . so too you should comfort mourners." (Sotah 14a)

In a remarkable statement in the Jerusalem Talmud, God is quoted as declaring: "If only they had abandoned Me, but kept My Torah" (Jerusalem Talmud, Hagigah 1:7). In other words, right conduct, as prescribed by the Torah, is paramount. Starting with the Torah and to the present day, Judaism has been action oriented. As David Wolpe writes: "What we do in this world is the real measure of any life."[8] Harold Schulweis adds: "Godliness is behaved. Godliness is believed through doing justice, in caring, in curing, in protecting. To behave in Godly fashion, is this not to know the divine?"[9]

JEWS, JUDAISM, AND THE LAND OF ISRAEL: AN ENDURING CONNECTION

It is a reality of historical research that there are far more sources to be found that describe more recent events than evidence that helps reconstruct the more distant past. From the Book of Genesis to the present day, Israel has loomed large in Jewish imagination, however large or small its Jewish population or the extent of its political sovereignty. Reflecting this historical association, Israel's Proclamation of Independences identifies the land of Israel as the birthplace of the

Jewish people; its spiritual, religious, and national identity took shape in Israel. "After being forcibly exiled from their land, the people remained faithful to it throughout their Dispersion and never ceased to pray and hope for their return and for the restoration of their national freedom."

Though historical uncertainties remain, it seems that, by three thousand years ago, a unified Israelite kingdom had been established, with its capital in Jerusalem. That kingdom split into two following the death of King Solomon, son and successor to King David. One kingdom, known as the kingdom of Judah, with its capital in Jerusalem, was ruled by the Davidic line; the other kingdom, known as Israel, had a succession of rulers who often established their family's rule for a period of generations before yielding to a more powerful, successor dynasty.

Israel, the northern kingdom, was conquered by the Assyrian empire in 722 BCE. Some Israelites fled to the kingdom of Judah; some were exiled. Others remained in their ancestral land but were culturally and religiously absorbed into the Assyrian way of life. The kingdom of Judah remained under Jewish rule until 586 BCE when it was overcome by Babylonia. In that year, the Temple in Jerusalem, constructed during the reign of King Solomon, was destroyed by the Babylonian invaders. Thousands of Judeans were exiled to Babylon, though the vast majority remained in Judea.

In time, Persia defeated Babylonia, and the Persian ruler, Cyrus, allowed Judeans interested in returning to their ancestral homeland to do so. Fifty years had elapsed since the Babylonian exile; only a few of the exiles (or children of exiled Judeans born in Babylonia) took up the offer of return. By 516 BCE, however, a Second Temple—authorized by Persian authorities—was rebuilt at the location of the earlier Temple built by King Solomon.

Persia's power gave way before the onslaught of Alexander the Great. Following Alexander's death, territory that he controlled, including Judea, was divided among several of his leading generals. For a long period, Judea was part of the empire of the Ptolemies, a Greek dynasty based in Egypt. In 198 BCE, it became part of the Syrian (Greek)-based Seleucid empire.

The area of which Judea was part was suffused with Hellenistic culture, a legacy of the Alexandrian conquest, extended Greek rule, and the pervasiveness of Hellenism. When in 167 BCE efforts—supported by some Judeans—were made to transform Jerusalem into a Greek polis (city), including the introduction of Greek religious rites, Judeans from the countryside rose up in revolt. The holiday of Hanukkah (literally, dedication) marks the rededication of the Temple by Judeans loyal to traditional Judean culture and Temple rituals, in 164 BCE, after the Syrian Greeks were routed from Jerusalem. War with the Seleucids continued for decades. Eventually, in about 140 BCE, Judea became an independent kingdom.

For the next century, Judea was ruled by a dynasty of kings descended from a family that had spearheaded the revolt against the Seleucids. The Hasmonean dynasty expanded its territory through military conquests, over the course of that century. At the same time, there were fissures within Judean society and a variety of Judean groups—differing in matters of religious interpretation and practice as well as political orientation—emerged.

Over time, the might of Rome extended to the Middle East. From 37 BCE to 4 BCE a Judean king—married, for a time, to a descendant of the Hasmonean family—ruled as a vassal of Rome. Herod, variously known as "the Great" and "the Wicked," built many structures that have survived to the present day. Eventually, Judea came to be ruled by a series of Roman-appointed procurators.

In the year 66 of the Common Era, a revolt against Roman authority was launched by Judean activists. The Romans defeated the insurgents, destroying the Second Temple (70 CE) in the process. Nonetheless, Judea remained the demographic center of Jewish life for more than another century.

It was a subsequent, unsuccessful, Judean rebellion, the Bar Kochba War of 132–135 CE, that led to harsh consequences resulting in the emigration of more and more Jews. In the aftermath of the Bar Kochba War the Roman emperor Hadrian renamed the province known as Judea; henceforth, it was to be called Syria Palaestina. The name was not altogether new; it was invoked, however, as the exclusive referent to the area to eviscerate any continuing linguistic association of the place with its Jewish antecedents.

By early in the third century, Babylonia seems to have supplanted Judea as the demographic center of Jewish life. The embrace of Christianity by the Roman empire caused further erosion of conditions of life for those Jews who remained in Judea. Christianity saw itself as the "new Israel," and there was little tolerance for those who clung to the "Old Testament," a covenant that Christianity viewed as having been abrogated and supplanted.

Although no longer the primary demographic center of Jewish population, the land of Israel remained central to the yearnings and rituals of Jews—who lived, variously, under Christian or Moslem rule—across the globe. Not only did prayers multiple times each day include the hope for the rebuilding of Jerusalem, restoration of the Davidic monarchy, and an ingathering of exiles, worshipers prayed in the direction of Jerusalem. Throughout the centuries, Jews remained in the area that, over time, came to be widely known as Palestine.

Writing in the twelfth century, Maimonides in his *Mishneh Torah*, Laws of Kings (11:1), envisions that a king will one day arise and renew the Davidic dynasty, rebuild the Temple in Jerusalem, and gather the dispersed of Israel. Accomplishing this will establish that that individual is, indeed, the messianic king. Maimonides continues: "The Sages and the prophets did not yearn for the Messianic era in order to have dominion over the entire world, to rule over the gentiles, to be exalted by the nations, or to eat, drink, and celebrate. Rather, they desired to be free to involve themselves in Torah and wisdom without any pressures or disturbances" (12:4).

FAST FORWARD: THE "OLD-NEW" STATE OF ISRAEL

Palestine was, for four hundred years (starting in 1516), part of the Ottoman empire. Though Jews continued to live in Palestine, most such residents—by the eighteenth and well into the nineteenth centuries—subsisted through charitable donations from Jewish communities abroad. During this period, modernizing trends expressed themselves in various parts of the world in greater or lesser measure.

In the United States and countries of Western Europe, Jews were accorded citizenship. In Russia, home to a plurality of the world's Jews in the nineteenth century (through annexation of parts of Poland), Jews pursued a variety of paths in response to modernizing trends that spread more gradually. The incursion of Western powers into parts of the Ottoman empire in the nineteenth century brought economic, cultural, and educational changes, with impact on Sephardic and Middle Eastern Jewry.

Many Jews were in search of Jewish meaning in an era of dramatic change and religious skepticism. Living at a time of rising nationalism, there were Jews who dreamed of building an ideal society rooted in socialist ideals or of "normalizing" Jewish life by returning to the land of Israel and working the soil. Some were simply seeking a safe haven in the face of rising anti-Semitism; others saw in Jewish life in Palestine the possibility of the cultural renewal of a Judaism in decay. Still others saw in the turmoil of the age the stirrings of messianic times ahead.

It was in this context that a movement to reclaim Jewish nationality in the land of Israel developed. Motivated by "love of Zion," tens of thousands of Jews—primarily, though not exclusively, from Russia—made *aliyah* (literally, ascent) to Israel in the decades before World War I. The Jewish population of Palestine increased from approximately 25,000 to 85,000 between 1881 and 1914.

Though Theodor Herzl was not the first to propose reclaiming Jewish nationality, his organizational initiative and leadership created a mechanism for effectively pursuing the aim of establishing a Jewish state. Herzl's publication, *The Jewish State* (1896), was followed by his convening a Zionist Congress (1897) and creating a Zionist Organization as a vehicle for pursuing collective objectives. Herzl and his successors sought the support of government authorities for recognition of an autonomous Jewish national home.

While Zionism represented continuity of the longstanding connection of Jews and Judaism with the land of Israel, it was discontinuous in refusing to passively await redemption at some indeterminate future time. For centuries, Jews had accepted exile as a reality that would continue until God redeemed them through messianic deliverance. Zionism sought redemption through human agency; it was, for the most part, a secular, nationalist initiative.[10]

From its inception, the Zionist movement was "home" to people of very divergent views (including Jews whose vision of national renewal was not necessarily tied to the land of Israel). For some, the primary agenda was ensuring the security of Jews; anti-Semitism made it essential to establish a safe refuge. For others, it was the crisis of Judaism—the need to create an opportunity for the regeneration of

Jewish culture—that was a driver. Still others were looking for religious fulfillment or to create a utopian society.

There were, in 1920, approximately five hundred thousand Arabs living in Palestine.[11] To the extent that Zionist thinkers—many of whom did not relocate to Palestine—considered this reality, it was generally with the view that Jewish immigration would bring improvements in living conditions to the benefit of all inhabitants. It was, therefore, imagined that Jewish settlement—on lands legally purchased—would be welcomed by local Arabs. As the Ottoman empire declined and was, eventually, ousted from Palestine, Arab national aspirations vied with those of the growing Jewish population of Palestine.

Tensions between local Arabs and the growing Jewish communities in Palestine escalated during the 1920s and 1930s, at a time when Great Britain—which had represented during World War I (publicly, through the Balfour Declaration) to Jews and (privately) to Arabs that it recognized their national aspirations—held a mandate (from the League of Nations) over Palestine. Zionist activism combined with heightened anti-Semitism in Europe and immigration restrictions in the United States and much of the Western world post–World War I, generated increased waves of Jewish immigration to Palestine. Riots of local Arabs against Jewish settlements erupted in 1921, 1929, and 1936. By 1939, 450,000 Jews and more than one million Arabs lived in Palestine.

Unable to reconcile the competing interests of Arabs and Jews, and amid further escalation of tensions post–World War II, Britain referred the problem of Palestine to the United Nations. On November 29, 1947, the General Assembly of the United Nations voted to partition Palestine into two states: a Jewish state and an Arab state. As the British Mandate drew to a close, David Ben-Gurion, head of the Jewish Agency—which had accepted the partition plan—proclaimed the establishment of the State of Israel on May 14, 1948. The armies of Lebanon, Syria, Iraq, Transjordan, and Egypt attacked on May 15 from the north, east, and south.

According to UN estimates, there were 726,000 Arab Palestinian refugees displaced in the course of the fighting.[12] Many of these individuals and families fled the scene of warfare—in some cases, forcibly—in the expectation of returning to their homes after the presumed victory of the invading Arab armies. The Israeli census of 1950 showed an Arab Israeli population of more than 150,000 within the new country.[13]

Though an armistice was reached and the State of Israel has flourished, regional tensions and the national aspirations of Palestinian Arabs remain unresolved three generations later. Exploration of the wars, negotiations, and efforts to address these enduring realities is beyond the scope of this introduction to the Torah and its central themes. It should, however, be noted that Israel and Egypt entered a peace treaty in 1979, followed by a peace treaty between Jordan and Israel in 1994.

In September 2020, the Abraham Accords, a declaration of mutual understanding in support of coexistence, friendly relations, and peace in the Middle East, accompanied by bilateral agreements between Israel and the United Arab Emirates and Israel and Bahrain, established diplomatic relations between Israel and two Arab Gulf States. Later that year, Israel and Morocco signed a normalization agreement establishing diplomatic relations. Sudan, too, signed the Abraham Accords; at this writing, a bilateral agreement with Israel, fully normalizing relations, remains pending.

Given the multiple visions that were, from the start, part of the modern Zionist project, it is no wonder that in the State of Israel there are more than a dozen political parties and that no single party has ever won a majority of seats in Israel's 120-member parliament (Knesset). Much has been written about the "Zionist idea" and the establishment, after two millennia, of a Jewish state in Israel.[14] What, however, is the significance of any of this for a Jew living outside the land of Israel in the third decade of the twenty-first century?

Writing in 1915, Louis Brandeis, who would soon (1916) become a justice of the US Supreme Court, affirmed that "every American Jew who aids in advancing the Jewish settlement in Palestine . . . will . . . be a better man and a better American for doing so." He continued: "Indeed, loyalty to America demands . . . that each American Jew become a Zionist. For only through the ennobling effect of its strivings can we develop the best that is in us and give to this country the full benefit of our great inheritance."[15]

Brandeis's comment is reminiscent of the passages in Genesis that point to Abraham as the progenitor of a particular people and, at the same time, a source of universal blessing. Through engagement with Israel and the constellation of themes that comprise the Torah, a Jew can enrich their experience as part of a particular people and share that people's wisdom with the communities of which they are part. The opportunity that Brandeis saw a century ago in working toward the establishment of a Jewish state in Israel is amplified in the era of Israel's sovereignty.

Though there are disagreements among demographers about population data, it appears that today 85 percent of the world's Jews live in Israel or the United States.[16] In the United States, Jews constitute 2.4 percent of the adult population.[17] In Israel, Jews comprise more than 73 percent of the country's inhabitants.[18]

Concern for the welfare of Jews living across the globe is part of *areivut*, a covenantal sense of mutual responsibility. That Israel is a sovereign Jewish state involves additional considerations. Israel's Proclamation of Independence (May 14, 1948)—as the British withdrew from Palestine, five and a half months following the UN decision to partition Palestine to a Jewish State and an Arab State—affirmed that "the State of Israel will be open to the immigration of Jews from all countries of their dispersion; will promote the development of the country for the benefit of all its inhabitants; will be based on the precepts of liberty, justice and peace taught by the Hebrew Prophets; will uphold the full social and political equality of all its citizens, without distinction of race, creed or sex; will guarantee full freedom of conscience, worship, education and culture; will safeguard the sanctity and inviolability of the shrines and Holy Places of all religions; and will dedicate itself to the principles of the Charter of the United Nations." The reality of a sovereign Jewish state committed to "the precepts . . . taught by the Hebrew Prophets" is far different from that of living as a Jew in any other setting.

During a visit to Israel a number of years ago, I visited the Supreme Court. As proceedings were open to the public, I entered a courtroom to get a sense of Israeli judicial procedure. To my fascination, the hearing I attended related to the claim of an Arab farmer who was petitioning the court to order the rerouting of a security fence recently placed, by government order, on his property, separating one portion of his land from another. While acknowledging state security interests, his claim was that security interests could be met by modifying placement of the security barrier. Though I don't know the resolution of that particular case, it represents one aspect of the unique circumstances of Jewish sovereignty. Reconciling public and private needs in a manner consistent with "the precepts . . . taught by the Hebrew prophets" is a matter that only arises in the State of Israel.

As the Torah manifests, there are often tensions between the ideal and the real. Israel must balance the aspiration to embody the ideals of the Prophets while navigating the existential realities of maintaining a nation-state that confronts very real security threats. There are complex issues about which Israeli citizens (Jews and Arabs alike) disagree. What, for example, should be the territorial borders of the state? What should be the relationship between church and state in the twenty-first-century sovereign State of Israel? What should be the balance of power between the elected, parliamentary government and the judiciary? From social welfare to military service, the exercise of power as a sovereign state, the ethics of war under a variety of circumstances, treatment of the "other," foreign relations, environmental policy, and more, the opportunity of applying Torah values to the conduct of civil society uniquely presents itself in a Jewish sovereign state.

As in the Torah there is considerable attention to visioning the sort of society to be established when the Israelites enter the land, ideas of what a Jewish nation-state might, in modern times, look like were and are much discussed. The project of building a society that can ensure the security of its citizens in a challenging environment and, at the same time, reflect the ideals articulated in the Proclamation of Independence is extraordinarily complex.[19] The demands of realpolitik and aspirational visions are often in tension. To relate to this project—both contributing to the security of the State of Israel and its pursuit of high ideals—even from a distance is a privilege that few generations of Jews have enjoyed.

Israel is a significant strand of contemporary Jewish conversation. It builds on a theme that harks back to the Torah. This short sketch is nothing more than an introduction. It remains for each individual who chooses to do so to fill in the blanks and take part in this dynamic aspect of a larger conversation. This dimension of Jewish expression is inextricably intertwined with others among the themes of the Torah, as we shall see.

Chapter 3

The Book of Exodus

Covenantal Responsibility;
Purpose in History

"History, as understood by the Torah," writes Rabbi Jonathan Sacks, "is the story of how human beings, led only by the sound of a voice, a call, began the long journey, not yet complete, to a promised land and a messianic age where people construct a society that honors the image of God in others, sanctifying life, building families of love and trust, shaping communities by the principles of justice and compassion, and living at peace with their neighbors." This narrative, Rabbi Sacks notes, "is saturated by the idea of covenant."[1] While the covenantal relationships of Genesis relate to individuals and families, Exodus—known in Hebrew as *Sh'mot* (names) because it opens with the names of the family of Jacob who came to reside in Egypt—turns to the saga of a people.

Abraham had been told that his offspring would be aliens in a land not their own and subjected to oppression for hundreds of years (Genesis 15:13). Jacob, in a night vision, hears God's assurance that He will descend with him to Egypt (Genesis 46:3). Joseph adjures his brothers to bring his bones with them when God restores the family to the land that He swore to Abraham, to Isaac, and to Jacob (Genesis 50:25). Exodus marks the beginning of the journey of return to the land of the patriarchs and matriarchs of Israel; it is a natural sequel to the Book of Genesis.

Bible scholar Nahum Sarna aptly observes that "the Torah is not a book of history, but one that makes use of historical data for didactic purposes."[2] "The biblical narratives," writes Sarna, are essentially documents of faith, not records of the past."[3] Identification with the experience of slavery, liberation from Egypt, God's presence at Sinai, and a journey toward the land of Israel hold a special place in Jewish collective memory. It is in the narrative of the Book of Exodus that the story of a people with a distinctive sense of purpose and vision of the future emerges.

Liberation from Egyptian slavery, the Torah conveys, was not simply for the sake of redemption from bondage. When Moses first experiences God's presence and hears himself summoned to serve as the agent of the Israelites' freedom, the sign he is given that his mission is, indeed, a Divine calling is that, when the people leave Egypt, they will encounter God at that very mountain (Exodus 3:12). In the words of Jonathan Sacks: "Freedom begins with exodus but it reaches its fulfillment in the acceptance of a code of conduct."[4] That code of conduct, set forth in the Torah, remains the subject of ongoing study, discussion, and application to life.

"Sinai," writes the late twentieth-century Jewish theologian David Hartman, "gave the community a direction, an arrow pointing toward a future filled with many surprises. *Halakhah* (Jewish law), which literally means 'walking,' is like a road that has not been fully paved and completed." Sinai represents an ongoing invitation to "one and all to acquire the competence to explore the terrain and extend the road."[5]

Historical details of the experiences of ancient Israel cannot be recaptured or recreated; archeological finds—and their absence—make for a variety of conjectures about the trajectory of biblical Israel among historians. The first external (to the Torah) reference to "Israel," referring to an ethnic group, is found on an Egyptian monument listing events thought to have occurred in 1207 BCE. Recording Pharaoh Merneptah's military successes against peoples in the Mediterranean, it notes (hyperbolically): "Israel is wasted; its seed is not."[6] Notwithstanding historical uncertainties, the narrative of the Book of Exodus serves, in the words of Rabbi Yitz Greenberg, as "an 'orienting event' . . . that sets in motion and guides the Jewish way (and, ultimately, humanity's way) toward the Promised Land—an earth set free and perfected."[7] Didactic memory (*zikaron*) of liberation from slavery and an encounter at Sinai has informed Jewish collective consciousness, nurturing a powerful sense of covenantal partnership toward realizing the ideal of a perfected world.

OPPRESSION IN EGYPT AND THE
ISRAELITES' LIBERATION FROM SLAVERY

Before turning to the enslavement of the Israelites early in the Book of Exodus, it is worthy of note that the servitude of a mass of people to Pharaoh is first referenced toward the end of the Book of Genesis. When famine drove the Egyptian people to desperation, Joseph—as Pharaoh's viceroy responsible for the granaries of Egypt—released grain to them in exchange for their horses, sheep, cattle, and donkeys (Genesis 47:16–17). As the famine continued and the people sought relief, Joseph acquired all their land for Pharaoh, in exchange for food; only the Egyptian priests retained their land. The rank-and-file Egyptians were, the Torah recounts, acquired with their land: Joseph said to the people, "I have this day acquired you and your land for Pharaoh, here is seed for you to sow the land" (Genesis 47:23).

Joseph directs that 20 percent of the crop be turned over to Pharaoh. The Egyptians recognize and express that they have become *avadim* (serfs, or slaves) to Pharaoh (Genesis 47:25). Devoted to the interests of Pharaoh—who was gracious to him and his extended family—Joseph, the Torah relates, facilitated the enslavement of masses of Egyptians to Pharaoh before a successor Pharaoh enslaved the descendants of Jacob who had settled in the land by invitation. One wonders whether this segment of the Joseph narrative is included as a cautionary tale.

The Pharaoh of the Book of Exodus expresses concern about the growing population and strength of the Israelites, aliens in Egypt. They could, he observes, potentially act as a fifth column in the event of war, joining with Egypt's enemies (Exodus 1:10). Though subjected to harsh labor, the Children of Israel continue to increase in number.

At that point, Pharaoh directs the midwives, Shiphrah and Puah, who attended to the Hebrew women, to kill male infants on the birth stool at the moment of birth. "The midwives, fearing God, did not do as the king of Egypt had told them; they let the boys live" (Exodus 1:17). Not only are these two women, unlike the all-powerful Pharaoh, referenced by name, "seven times in this brief episode the term 'midwife' is repeated, an index of the importance that Scripture places upon the actions of the women in their defiance of tyranny and in their upholding of moral principles. Here we have history's first recorded case of civil disobedience in defense of a moral cause."[8]

Failing to surreptitiously accomplish his annihilation plan, Pharaoh orders that all Israelite male newborns be thrown into the Nile River. The Torah relates that a man and woman of the house of Levi produced a son. The mother hid the child for a time, and when she could no longer conceal him she took a wicker basket, smeared it with clay and pitch, placed the child in the ark (the same word, *tevah*, is used in reference to Noah's vessel; in each case, the *tevah* is a vehicle of salvation), and put it among the reeds at the river bank (Exodus 2:3). The infant's sister, Miriam, stations herself nearby and is present when none other than Pharaoh's daughter spots the crying child and, with pity, says: "This must be a Hebrew child" (Exodus 2:6).

The infant's sister offers to find a wet nurse for the child, and following this encounter, Pharaoh's daughter ends up enlisting the child's mother as his nurse. At some point—presumably, when he is weaned—the child goes to live with Pharaoh's daughter. It is she who names him Moses, "for I drew him out of the water" (Exodus 2:10). In rapid succession—starting with the midwives Shiphrah and Puah and proceeding to Moses's mother, sister, and adoptive mother, Pharaoh's daughter—women play a leading role in the unfolding drama leading toward the Israelites' liberation from Egypt.

Moses, who is aware of his Hebrew identity—the biblical narrative indicates that he "went out to his kinsfolk and witnessed their labors" (Exodus 2:11)—sees an Egyptian strike a Hebrew man of his brethren. Moses strikes the Egyptian and hides him in the sand (Exodus 2:12). When, the following day, Moses sees a Hebrew man strike another Hebrew and asks the perpetrator why he is doing so, the aggressor replies: "Who made you chief and ruler over us? Do you mean to kill me, as you killed the Egyptian?" (Exodus 2:14). Recognizing that his deed is common knowledge, Moses flees to the territory of the Midianites.

No sooner does Moses arrive at a well in Midian than he sees a group of women pushed aside from the watering trough by male shepherds. Notwithstanding the experiences that have led him to this faraway place and the fact that he has no relationship to any of the actors in the scene he has witnessed, "Moses rose to their defense, and he watered their flock" (Exodus 2:17). The women are the daughters of the priest of Midian; Moses, their rescuer, is invited to the home of the Midianite priest, and he eventually marries Zipporah, one of the daughters of his host.

That, of all that might have transpired in Moses's life from the time he entered the royal household until he married in Midian, the Torah relates these three episodes serve to emphasize Moses's commitment to justice. Whether the presenting issue was the abuse of one of his perceived brethren, a dispute between two of his brethren, or an injustice between total strangers, Moses feels compelled to act. Perhaps this quality rendered Moses particularly well suited to the task ahead.

Rabbinic tradition adds to the image of Moses as a man of justice the trait of compassion. A midrash relates that "once, while Moses was tending (his father-in-law) Jethro's sheep, one of the sheep ran away. Moses ran after it until it reached a small, shaded place. There, the lamb came across a pool and began to drink. As Moses approached the lamb, he said 'I did not know you ran away because you were thirsty. You are so exhausted!' He then put the lamb on his shoulders and carried him back. The Holy One said, 'Since you tend the sheep of human beings with such compassion, you shall be the shepherd of My sheep, Israel'" (Exodus Rabbah 2:2).

It is in the course of tending Jethro's flock that Moses sees the spectacle of a bush that seems ablaze but is not consumed. The sight of the bush attracts him; Moses thereupon hears a voice—the God of Abraham, the God of Isaac—summoning him to go to Pharaoh to "free My people, the Israelites, from Egypt" (Exodus 3:10). As earlier indicated, the sign that this mission is on the "up and up," records the Torah narrative, is that "when you have freed the people from Egypt, you shall serve God on this mountain" (Exodus 3:12).

Moses is reluctant to undertake this project, indicating, among other things, that he is not a man of words; he declines five times. Aaron, Moses's brother, he is told, is about to meet him; "You shall speak to him and put the words in his mouth—I will be with you and with him as you speak, and tell both of you what to do" (Exodus 4:15). Since Moses's flight from Egypt, the Pharaoh of his formative years died. Although a new ruler is now in power, the burden and cry of the children of Israel are great (Exodus 2:23). Perhaps the Israelites had harbored hope that, with the ascent of a new Pharaoh, conditions would improve; this did not, however, prove to be the case. It is to the new Pharaoh that Moses and Aaron will present themselves on behalf of the Israelites.

TOWARD EXODUS FROM EGYPT:
THE TEN PLAGUES

Following his experience at the burning bush, Moses takes leave—
with his wife and sons—of his father-in-law and heads toward Egypt.
En route, Moses meets Aaron "at the mountain of God" and tells him
"about all the things that the Lord had committed to him" (Exodus
4:27–28). Moses and Aaron assemble the elders of the Israelites. Aaron
addresses them and demonstrates signs that God had shown Moses; the
elders are convinced that God has taken notice of their plight and that
liberation is at hand.

The initial appearance of Moses and Aaron in Pharaoh's court follows
their successful encounter with the Israelite elders. They request, in the
name of the God of Israel, that the Hebrews be granted the opportunity
of celebrating a festival to their God, traveling a distance of three days'
journey into the wilderness. Pharaoh's immediate response is: "Who
is the Lord that I should heed Him and let Israel go? I do not know
the Lord, nor will I let Israel go" (Exodus 5:2). Moreover, he directs
that, without diminishing from the quota of daily brick production, the
Hebrew slaves should gather straw that had hitherto been provided. The
slaves, apparently, had too much time on their hands; hence, such talk
of going to the wilderness to serve their God.

Nehama Leibowitz, in her work on the Book of Exodus, explores the
question of whether the request for a three-day journey was a deception.
Quoting Don Isaac Abarbanel (1437–1508), she interprets it as an hon-
est request. Were Pharaoh to have acceded to that limited request, the
Israelites would have returned to Egypt after the prescribed time, and
Moses would have continued negotiations for their release.[9]

Moses, reluctant to undertake the mission from the outset, remonstrates with God: "Why did You send me? Ever since I came to Pharaoh
to speak in Your name, he has dealt worse with this people; and still
You have not delivered Your people" (Exodus 5:22–23). God replies
that Pharaoh will not only let them go, "he shall drive them from his
land" (Exodus 6:1). Yet when Moses and Aaron convey to the Israelites
God's message that redemption is at hand and that God will bring the
Israelites to the land of their ancestors—Abraham, Isaac, and Jacob—
the Israelites do not listen; they are utterly demoralized.

When Moses and Aaron next appear before Pharaoh, they perform a sign that they had earlier demonstrated to the elders of the Israelites. Aaron casts down his rod, and it turns into a serpent. Pharaoh's magicians, in turn, replicate this feat. Aaron's rod, however, swallows those of the magicians. However, "Pharaoh's heart stiffened" (Exodus 7:13). It is following this encounter that the plagues unfold.

Nahum Sarna notes that in chapters 4 through 14 of the Book of Exodus, there are twenty references to the hardening of Pharaoh's heart: "Ten times it is said that the pharaoh hardened his own heart, and ten times the hardening is attributed to God."[10] In his *Mishneh Torah* (Laws of Repentance 6:2), Maimonides notes that free will is foundational to the possibility of repentance. However, an ongoing pattern of wicked conduct eliminates the possibility of exercising free will; an individual is ensnared by an ongoing pattern of choices earlier, freely, made. Consistent with this view, it is only with the sixth plague that there is attribution to God of hardening Pharaoh's heart; by then, Pharaoh had become entrenched in a course of conduct from which he could no longer extricate himself.

In a late twentieth-century work, Rabbi Harold Schulweis notes that many classical commentaries focus on the spiritual meaning and moral significance of seemingly miraculous events. "Symbolic explanations," writes Schulweis, "flow from the rabbinic moral conviction that, 'Whatever measure a man metes out shall be measured to him again.'" In such a reading, "the attention to the plagues focuses on their moral symmetry."[11] Through such a lens, for example, the Nile River turning to blood might represent symbolic punishment for the drowning of Israelite boys.

After Egypt encounters plagues of blood (rather than water) in the Nile River, frogs, lice, insects, pestilence, boils, and hail, Pharaoh's courtiers urge him to permit the Israelites to go worship their God. Pharaoh summons Moses and Aaron and asks whom they propose to take on the worship journey. Moses replies, "We will all go, young and old: we will go with our sons and daughters, our flocks and herds; for we must observe the Lord's festival" (Exodus 10:9). Proclaiming that it is only the men whom he would permit to go worship, Pharaoh dismisses Moses and Aaron from his presence. Locusts, followed by darkness, plague the Egyptians. After three days of thick darkness, Pharaoh summons Moses and expresses readiness to allow all the Israelites to go worship: "Only your flocks and your herds shall be left behind; even your children may go with you" (Exodus 10:24). This, too, is rejected by Moses, at which point Pharaoh indicates that he will negotiate no further.

THE MONTH OF LIBERATION

Before turning to the last plague and Pharaoh's subsequent capitulation, the biblical text relates that "this month shall mark for you the beginning of the months; it shall be the first of the months of the year for you" (Exodus 12:2). Control of time is the beginning of the road to freedom. Historian Elisheva Carlebach aptly notes that "one of the most crucial cultural monuments a human society can create is a system of accounting for time."[12] It is instructive that, based on Exodus 12:2, determination of the onset of each Hebrew calendar month would involve direct observation and testimony about the moon, processed and pronounced by the High Court (Sanhedrin) in Jerusalem. Human beings, partners in the covenant, would interpret observable data to reckon the start of each month and thereby determine when various holidays would be observed.

Time and again, and in various ways, Jewish tradition relates to the reality that, though the world transcends human design, people play an essential role in shaping its realities. The *Midrash Tanḥuma* (*Tazria* 5), a work compiled in the eighth and ninth centuries, relates that, responding to questions posed by the Roman governor-general Turnus Rufus about the powers of God and humankind, Rabbi Akiba brought his interlocutor stalks of wheat and a loaf of bread and declared: "These are the works of the Holy One Blessed is He, and these are the works of man." While the loaves of bread are, surely, more delectable, the capacity of humankind to refine the wheat depends on preexisting conditions. The world is not of human design, but bread emerges from God's world only through the agency of human intervention.

While human intervention can refine, in positive ways, the natural order of the world, the misuse of human freedom can lead to horrific outcomes. As David Hartman comments, "Failure, uncertainty, and unpredictability are permanent features of life under the covenant, since human freedom is constitutive of the covenantal relationship."

The covenant that the Israelites will enter as a free people "teaches the community how to be responsible for its social and political existence even within the uncertain and possibly tragic conditions of history and even though many events are beyond human control."[13]

Instructions instituting a new calendar are followed, in Exodus 12:3ff, by a description of preparations to be taken in anticipation of leaving Egypt, starting with a paschal offering prepared and eaten by each household. In addition to the paschal offering, the Israelites are to eat matzah, an instruction supplemented by a prohibition of retaining or eating leavened bread. The Passover meal is also to include bitter herbs. The Israelites are instructed to daub some of the blood of the paschal offering on the doorposts and lintel of their houses so that they would be protected from the plague that will soon be visited on the Egyptians.

During the night of the fifteenth of the first month, the first-born in the land of Egypt—whose Pharaoh had planned the annihilation of all Israelite male newborns—are struck down; "there was no house where there was not someone dead" (Exodus 12:30). Pharaoh summons Moses and Aaron and urges that they and their people, with their flocks and herds, be gone (Exodus 12:31). Honoring the oath that the children of Israel had sworn to Joseph centuries earlier, Moses takes the bones of Joseph, as the Israelites depart Egypt (Exodus 13:19).

As the Israelites proceed toward *Yam Suf* (literally, Sea of Reeds), Pharaoh has a change of heart and pursues the Israelites with a corps of six hundred chariots. With the sea in front of them and the Egyptians drawing near, the Israelites turn to Moses, asking: "Was it for want of graves in Egypt that you brought us to die in the wilderness? What have you done to us, taking us out of Egypt?" (Exodus 14:11).

The biblical text tells of a strong east wind that parts the sea; the Israelites are able to proceed. The pursuing Egyptians, immobilized as their chariots become bogged down in the mud, decide to retreat. The sea, however, returns to its normal state, and the Egyptians are hurled into the waters. "Israel saw the Egyptians dead on the shore of the sea. And when Israel saw the wondrous power which the Lord had wielded against the Egyptians, the people feared the Lord; they had faith in the Lord and His servant Moses" (Exodus 14:30–31).

It is interesting to note that the verb "to see" that appears in these verses is in the singular form (*va-yar*). The Israelites beheld "as one" the identical phenomena. The text continues by noting that the people had awe of the Lord's power and placed trust in the Lord and the Lord's servant Moses. Yet the verbs for fear (or awe) and faith (*va-yiru, va-ya'aminu*) are in plural form. Multiple people can, collectively, see a singular phenomenon, but the manner in which their observations are individually processed is not uniform.

What follows is a song of praise, rhetorically asking: "Who is like You, O Lord, among the celestials; Who is like You, majestic in holiness, Awesome in splendor, working wonders!" (Exodus 15:11). It concludes with the affirmation "the Lord will reign for ever and ever" (Exodus 15:18). Not only do Moses and the children of Israel sing of God's might, Miriam the prophetess, timbrel in hand, leads the women in dance and song (Exodus 15:20–21). The Talmud relates that the angels, too, broke into song. God, however, responded: "How can you sing when the works of my hand are drowning in the sea?" (Megillah 10b; Sanhedrin 39b).

Notwithstanding the circumstances of their liberation from Egypt and the celebration of deliverance in which all Israel joined, the realities of life in the desert—with attendant shortages of water and food—lead to bitter complaints. The Israelites complain to Moses: "If only we had died by the hand of the Lord in the land of Egypt, when we sat by the fleshpots, when we ate our fill of bread! For you have brought us out into this wilderness to starve this whole congregation to death" (Exodus 16:3). Time and again, God responds to the people's expressed needs, notwithstanding their persistent ingratitude. Nahum Sarna comments that "this is significant because one of the cardinal principles of biblical theology is *imitatio dei*, 'the imitation of God,' the obligation of humankind to emulate, where possible, divine attributes—in the present instance, forbearance under provocation, empathy, magnanimity, and caring for the needy and the hungry."[14]

APPROACHING SINAI

Proceeding on their journey, the recently freed slaves are attacked from the rear by Amalek, a tribe of desert nomads that strikes weak stragglers without cause (Deuteronomy 25:17–19 adds further details to the account of Exodus 17:8–16). Joshua leads Israelite forces into battle. "Then, whenever Moses held up his hand, Israel prevailed; but whenever he let down his hand, Amalek prevailed" (Exodus 17:11). The *Mekhilta*, an early midrashic work, understands this to mean that when the people turned their faces heavenward and had faith, they prevailed; when their faith flagged, so did their success on the battlefield.

The successful battle with Amalek is followed, in the Book of Exodus, by a visit of Moses's father-in-law, Jethro (Yitro), to the Israelite camp. Arriving with his daughter and grandsons not long after the Israelites' emergence from Egypt, Yitro observes Moses's daily activity. From morning to evening, people come to him with disputes requiring resolution.

Jethro, a Midianite priest and stranger to the camp, recognizes that such an approach to the judicial function is untenable: "The thing you are doing is not right; you will surely wear yourself out, and these people as well. For the task is too heavy for you; you cannot do it alone" (Exodus 18:17–18). Moses heeds his father-in-law's advice and appoints "chiefs of thousands, hundreds, fifties, and tens; and they judged the people at all times: the difficult matters they would bring to Moses, and all the minor matters they would decide themselves" (Exodus 18:25–26). Moses taught by his example that all can learn from the wisdom of others, even from the priest of a foreign god. In the words of the second-century teacher Ben Zoma: "Who is wise? The one who learns from every person" (Avot 4:1).

Yitro's counsel to Moses comes between the battle with Amalek and the encounter at Sinai. Having been enslaved by the Egyptians and attacked by the Amalekites, the Israelites might have concluded that all non-Israelites are enemies or oppressors. Yitro, who rejoices at the good that the Israelites had experienced, evidences that this is not the case. On the threshold of receiving instruction at Sinai, the Israelites are reminded through Yitro of the great gift of intellect with which all people are endowed. Reason and Torah are both gifts to be celebrated.[15]

It is at Sinai, the Torah relates, that Moses hears God's call from the mountain instructing him to tell the Israelites that "if you will obey Me faithfully and keep My covenant, you shall be My treasured possession. . . . You shall be to Me a kingdom of priests and a holy nation" (Exodus 19:5–6). Becoming a kingdom of priests and a holy nation is nothing less than the mission statement of the Jewish people.

The commandments of Sinai—the laws of the Torah—are presented as the terms of a Divine covenant with the people Israel. By way of response, the Torah continues, "All the people answered as one, saying, 'All that the Lord has spoken we will do!'" (Exodus 19:8). This covenantal commitment not only connects the people to the charge they have accepted, it establishes a collective purpose linking them with one another.

Rabbi Jonathan Sacks notes that in premodern societies, priests held a virtual monopoly on literacy. The word "hieroglyphic," he observes, means priestly script. Similarly, the double meaning of "clerical," referring to clergy and to clerks, harks back to the Middle Ages, when religious functionaries were the educated class. That all Israel is instructed to be a "kingdom of priests," suggests Sacks, bespeaks an educational imperative devolving on all members of Israelite society; it means a society of universal literacy.[16]

Nahum Sarna points to the interweaving of spiritual, cultic, moral, and legal demands in the Decalogue and beyond as "one of the quintessential, differentiating characteristics of biblical law." While "all other systems in the ancient world display an atomistic approach to life," biblical law is holistic; "it is not compartmentalized." Accordingly, "an offense against sexual morality, against business morality, against social morality, is simultaneously a 'religious' offense because, one and all, they are infractions of the divine will."[17] It is through adherence to the laws of the Torah—requiring education of successive generations—that Israel is to be a "kingdom of priests and a holy nation."

Sarna's observation about the holistic nature of the laws of the Torah is reflected in the range of laws that comprise the Ten Commandments (literally, the ten statements). The first group of commandments consists of obligations unique to Israelite religion: the worship of one God, the prohibition against idolatry, and maintaining the Sabbath manifest the unique relationship between God and the Israelites. A second group within the Ten Commandments regulates interpersonal relationships. Their uniqueness as part of the Torah is the fact that they are presented as expressions of the Divine will. Reflecting the relationships with God and with human beings that begin and end the Decalogue, the text starts with "I the Lord am your God" (Exodus 20:2) and closes with "your neighbor's" (Exodus 20:14).

The statements of the Decalogue are presented in apodictic style, "You shall" or "You shall not"; penalties for infractions are not set forth. Sarna notes that these matters are not by coincidence. "They declare that there are certain God-given values and behavioral norms that are absolute. Morality is the expression of the divine will. The motivation for observing the law is not fear of punishment but the desire to conform to the will of God."[18]

THE BOOK OF THE COVENANT: RULES OF LAW (EXODUS 21–24)

Chapters 21 through 24 of Exodus are composed of a collection of laws that Moses sets before the Israelites. Many of these laws deal with civil and criminal matters, including such topics as treatment of slaves, torts, homicide, and bailment. Some are case law, arising out of real or hypothetical situations; some are commandments or statements of obligation. This body of law opens with the conjunction "and." (And) "these are the rules that you shall place before them" (Exodus 21:1). Rashi comments that just as the preceding commandments were given at Sinai, so were these; hence, the conjunction "and." Relating to the phrase "that you shall place before them," Rashi suggests that Moses was to teach not only the laws but the principles and rationales underlying them.

"Torah law" extends well beyond the laws that appear in the Torah text. The Talmud relates that Moses was accorded the opportunity of visiting the study hall of Rabbi Akiba, a leading rabbinic authority of the late first/early second century CE. In this imaginative account, Moses sits in a back row and is unable to follow the discussion. At a certain point, a disciple of Akiba asks his teacher, "'From whence do you know it?' and the latter replies, 'it is a law given to Moses at Sinai'" (Menaḥot 29b). Drawing out the implications and applications of Torah—the written text and oral tradition—is also, this story conveys, Torah. As the medieval Jewish thinker Joseph Albo (1380–1444) explains: "Moses was given orally at Sinai only general principles, only briefly alluded to in the Torah, by means of which the wise men in every generation may work out the details as they appear" (*Sefer Ha-Ikkarim*, Book Three, section 23).[19]

In a book titled *A Living Tree: The Roots and Growth of Jewish Law*, Professors Elliot Dorff and Arthur Rosett note that "the rabbinic tradition of interpretation starts with supreme confidence that, however subtle the text may be, somewhere within it correct guidance on every legal issue can be found. The text itself may appear repetitive, obscure, incomplete, or inconsistent, but all the seeming problems just show the need for explanation. The text is authentic, complete and correct; it is just our ability to read and understand it that is limited."[20] Many competing interpretations are possible, and rabbinic legal discussions often preserve minority viewpoints.

The oral law, eventually recorded, starting early in the third century, was seen by the rabbis as part and parcel of the Torah of Sinai. The *tannaim* and *amoraim*—rabbis of the Mishnah and the more expanded discussion known as the Gemara; collectively, the Talmud—interpreted and applied legal passages of the Torah. Through such exegesis, writes theologian Louis Jacobs, "Israel, the covenant people, tries to discover God's will in order to obey it."[21]

Among many examples of the elucidation of the laws of the Torah in the oral tradition is the Mishnah's formulation giving expression to the case described in Exodus 21:18–19. The Torah text reads: "When men quarrel and one strikes the other with stone or fist, and he does not die but has to take to his bed—if he then gets up and walks outdoors upon his staff, the assailant shall go unpunished, except that he must pay for his idleness and his cure." The Mishnah details the measure of liability: for the injury itself, for pain, for medical expenses, for absence from work, and for humiliation/mental anguish (Bava Kamma 83b). Similarly, "eye for eye" (Exodus 21:24) was interpreted as requiring monetary compensation (Bava Kamma 83b–84a).

Interspersed with the extensive series of laws in these chapters are several reminders to consider the plight of the alien. By way of example, "You shall not wrong a stranger or oppress him, for you were strangers in the land of Egypt" (Exodus 22:20); "You shall not oppress a stranger, you know the feelings of a stranger, having yourselves been strangers in the land of Egypt" (Exodus 23:9). Concern for the welfare and rights of the stranger is referenced thirty-six times in the Torah. It is an expression of the impact that the collective memory of slavery in Egypt is to exercise upon the Israelites and their descendants.

INSTRUCTIONS FOR BUILDING
THE TABERNACLE (*MISHKAN*)

Chapters 25 through 31 of the Book of Exodus present instructions for building a portable tabernacle, or sanctuary. Many commentators have noted that construction of the sanctuary is not described as causing God's Presence to enter the sanctuary but, rather, to dwell amid the people. Commenting on Exodus 25:8, Samson Raphael Hirsch suggests that when the people Israel sanctifies itself, represented in this instance by construction of the *mishkan*, God will dwell among them.[22]

All Israel is invited to contribute to the tabernacle's construction: "Tell the Israelite people to bring Me gifts; you shall accept gifts for Me from every person whose heart so moves him" (Exodus 25:2). Numerous accoutrements of the tabernacle are detailed, with instructions to Moses framed in the singular: "*ve-asita*" (and you—singular—shall make). The instruction to build the ark (Exodus 25:10) is, however, expressed in the plural: "*ve-asu*" (and they shall make). Because the ark contained the Ten Commandments, it was essential that the entire community be associated with its construction; no single person should be in a position to lay exclusive claim to Torah. As the experience at Sinai was a collective experience, so would the tabernacle involve the entirety of the people Israel.

Nahum Sarna comments that portable shrines were "well rooted in the cultural and religious traditions of the ancient Near East." Yet "the essential ideas that are enshrined in the Tabernacle and the religious concepts that it expresses are wholly Israelite and radically different from its compares."[23] Most conspicuously different from pagan temples was the "ark of the covenant." While, in pagan shrines, the innermost sanctum housed the image of a god, in the Israelite tabernacle "in place of the representation of the deity came the tangible symbol of His Word—the stone tablets of the Covenant."[24] The very idea of a covenant or legal agreement between a deity and a people was unique to Israel.

At the close of the instructions for constructing the *mishkan*, Moses is directed to remind the Israelites of the imperative of observing the Sabbath. Based on the phrase, "Nevertheless, you must keep My sabbaths" (Exodus 31:13), the sages derived the prohibited creative activities of Shabbat from the tasks involved in building the tabernacle (Mishnah Shabbat 7:2). The word "nevertheless" (*akh*) is also interpreted, however, to indicate that there are exceptions to the rule stated; thus, for example, the qualification that one should violate the Sabbath to save a life.

EXODUS 32–34: THE GOLDEN CALF
AND ITS AFTERMATH

Between instructions for building the *mishkan* and the description of actually constructing the tabernacle, the biblical text presents the episode of the golden calf. Moses had served as the mediator between God and the Israelites. When Moses ascends Sinai and does not return after forty days, the people turn to Aaron in search of an intermediary. Not knowing what had become of Moshe *ha-ish*—the man Moses—"who brought us from the land of Egypt," they gather and demand of Aaron, "Come, make us a god who shall go before us" (Exodus 32:1).

Rather than the word of God—represented in the imagery of the tablets of law in the holy of holies—as the manifestation of the divine presence, a material symbol of God is demanded. Aaron instructs the people in fashioning a golden calf. The people bring offerings; they eat and drink and rise to dance (Exodus 32:6). God shares with Moses a sense of what has transpired and proposes to wipe out the Israelites, starting a nation anew with Moses and his descendants. Moses intercedes on the people's behalf.

Moses descends the mountain, bearing tablets of law with God's writing "incised [*harut*] upon the tablets" (Exodus 32:16). The Torah text is not vocalized, and the Hebrew letters spelling *harut*, incised or engraved, can also be read as *herut*, freedom. Homiletically, it has been suggested that genuine freedom is not achieved through the absence of rules but rather by seeking to understand and give expression in action to meeting divine expectations.

Joshua, who had accompanied Moses part way, meets Moses, and they hear boisterousness in the camp of Israel. As Moses beholds the calf and the dancing, he hurls the tablets of law he had carried from the mountain. They shatter at the foot of the mountain.

It is at the close of this episode that Moses asks to behold God's presence. He is told that no man can behold God; the mystery of the divine reality can never be fully apprehended (Exodus 33:19–23). As he ascends the mountain a second time, bearing tablets like the ones he had earlier broken, Moses's request to know God's ways (Exodus 33:13) is partially answered when such attributes as compassion and graciousness are proclaimed (Exodus 34:6–7).

Maimonides, in his Code of Jewish Law (*Mishneh Torah*, Book of Knowledge, Ethical Ideas 1:6), draws upon the Talmud (Shabbat 133b) for the proposition that humankind is to strive to imitate God in these traits. Maimonides continues (Ethical Ideas 1:7): "And since the Creator is referred to by these attributes . . . this path is called the way of God. Our forefather Abraham taught it to his children, as it is said [of Abraham] 'that he may instruct his children and his posterity to keep the way of the Lord by doing what is just and right'" (Genesis 18:19).

EXODUS 35–40: CONSTRUCTION OF THE TABERNACLE

Moses returns to the Israelite camp a second time, his face radiant, bearing two inscribed tablets of law, reflecting renewal of the covenant. The earlier-described project of constructing the tabernacle is now launched. Bezalel and Oholiab, the outstanding craftsmen directing the project, are described as knowledgeable and inspired artisans possessing the ability to instruct others. Ibn Ezra (1089–1167) comments that there are scholars who have considerable wisdom but are lacking in the capacity to teach; for this reason, the Torah specifically notes that Bezalel and Oholiab had both skill and the ability to effectively educate others.

Bezalel was from the tribe of Judah, the largest of the tribes; Oholiab was from Dan, the smallest of the tribes. All Israel was to be represented in this project. Nahum Sarna observes that the account of building the *mishkan* includes many phrases echoing the creation narrative. For example, the statement in Genesis 2:1, "The heaven and the earth were finished, and all their array," is paralleled by, "Thus was completed all the work of the Tabernacle of the Tent of Meeting" (Exodus 39:32). "The tabernacle," Sarna comments, "was conceived to initiate a new era in the life of the community of Israel, and the rites that were performed in it thereafter afforded every Israelite the possibility of spiritual renewal and moral regeneration."[25]

A cloud covered the tabernacle; "When the cloud lifted from the Tabernacle, the Israelites would set out, on their various journeys" (Exodus 40:36). The Book of Exodus instructs that the people Israel is to be a "holy nation." Alongside the journey to the Promised Land is a journey toward *kedushah*, holiness. It is to that theme that the Torah will next turn.

Chapter 4

History, Covenant, and a Vision of the Future

In his book *Basic Judaism*, Milton Steinberg aptly explains that "to Judaism history is the unfolding of a design the denouement of which is to be man's ultimate fulfillment and redemption."[1] Will Herberg observes that no Greek historians "showed any sign of believing that the doings of men in time were . . . somehow significant for the destiny of mankind." To the contrary: "To the Greeks, humankind had no destiny. The strivings and doings of men, their enterprises, conflicts and achievements, led nowhere. All, all would be swallowed up in the cycle of eternal recurrence that was the law of the cosmos."[2] In juxtaposition to this perspective, the Hebrew Bible sees history as a purposeful process.

Jonathan Sacks points out that while other civilizations harked back to a glorious, mythical past, Judaism was and remains future oriented; it recognizes that the future is not destined to be like the past. "History," he writes, "is not an endless series of eternal recurrences or *deja vus*. Indeed it is like a journey, with a starting point and a destination, or like a book with a beginning and middle and distantly glimpsed end."[3] Endowed with free will, human beings are "co-authors in writing the script of history."[4]

Central to the Book of Exodus is a covenantal relationship. The Israelites are to be a "kingdom of priests," fulfilling their part of the covenant through living in ways that give expression to the values and instructions of Torah. As Abraham was to "be a blessing," so are the Jewish people, individually and collectively, to contribute to the well-being of humankind.

David Lieber well describes the impact of the sense of covenantal mission on the people Israel: "The conviction that God had entered into a covenant with its ancestors shaped Israel's entire worldview. It taught the Israelites that God cares about human beings, particularly for those who, like the people of ancient Israel, were helpless and oppressed. The covenant also made it plain that Israel's election was not for Israel's sake but to serve God's purpose for the rest of the world. It entailed obligation, not special privilege."[5]

In his book *A Living Covenant*, David Hartman takes note that "human freedom is constitutive of the covenantal relationship"; given free will and human coauthorship of history, there is no guarantee—as is all too apparent—that history is secure against humankind's misuse of freedom.[6] Yet as Jonathan Sacks comments, "With God's help and that of the people with whom we are bound in covenant, we can change the world."[7]

Torah and engagement with it are not static. When the Torah is read during synagogue services, individuals honored by being called up (*aliyah*; ascending) recite a blessing before and after the reading of passages from the Torah scroll. The blessings refer to God giving—in the present—the Torah. Torah, the declarant affirms, is continuously received and interpreted.

Tamar Ross, professor emerita in the Department of Philosophy at Bar Ilan University, comments that "God does not speak through vocal chords"; rather, revelation is a process. "This process," she writes, "began with the formal canonization of the Torah and its acceptance by the Jewish people. . . . It continues . . . with the cumulative interpretations that accrue to this text, inevitably informing and altering its meaning in light of the ever-changing historical contexts in which it is read." Accordingly, Ross suggests, for the religious thinker, "the Torah can be understood as all human (in terms of its literary and historical genesis) and all divine (in terms of its origin, value, and significance) at one and the same time."[8]

It is worthy of note that the Hebrew root for "giving," *ntn*, is a palindrome. There is a reciprocal relationship between giving and receiving reflected in the word itself. Though Torah is viewed by many Jews as the expression of God's Will, its recipients are human beings whose understanding and application of Torah endow it with mediated meaning.

In a well-known Talmudic passage (Bava Metzia 59a–59b) in which early second-century rabbinic sages are debating whether a particular type of earthenware oven is susceptible to ritual impurity, the lone proponent of a minority position on the matter at issue calls upon a heavenly voice to confirm that his view is correct. In response, a heavenly voice proclaims to those in the council of rabbis holding the majority view: "Why do you dispute with Rabbi Eliezer, seeing that in all matters the law agrees with him?" One of the council, Rabbi Joshua, responds by quoting the Torah for the proposition that "it is not in Heaven" (Deut. 30:12). Because the Torah instructs that the majority is to be followed (Exodus 23:2), the heavenly voice has no standing. Interpretation and application of the Torah to life is relegated to humankind.

A central expression of covenantal living is translating the ideals of Torah to concrete actions through the performance of *mitzvot*, sacred obligations (literally, commandments). Eliezer Berkovits, a twentieth-century Jewish philosopher, defines *halakhah* (literally, way; commonly translated as Jewish law) as the application of Torah to life. "But since there is no such thing as life in general, since it is always a certain form of life at a specific time of history, Torah application means application to a specific time, in a specific situation."[9] Emanuel Rackman, a contemporary of Berkovits, observes:

> No one familiar with Talmudic literature can help but marvel at the ingenuity, nay, the audacity, of the creators of that literature to modify God's word. Indeed, though they were collaborators with God in interpreting His revelations—His Torah—it would appear that they were not junior partners. Often they found an irrelevant text to support their deed but more often than not, they relied upon the values system of the traditions and sometimes they went beyond that and embraced values of their own and of the world about them.[10]

As Tamar Ross notes, "given Judaism's powerful commitment to the belief in a righteous God whose Torah is Just, it is both valid and appropriate that moral concerns play an important part in creating the need for new interpretation and in its formulation."[11] In that spirit, standards of correct behavior set forth in the Torah are viewed as minimum requirements with the expectation that adherents will act beyond the requirements of law. Discussing why Jerusalem was destroyed, the Talmud records the view that destruction resulted from the Jews judging (only) according to the law of the Torah: "They insisted on the law of the Torah and did not act above and beyond the strict requirement of the law (*lifnim mishurat ha-din*)" (Bava Metzia 30b).

Sharing, with Berkovits, Rackman, and Ross, abiding respect for *halakhah* (Jewish law), Walter Wurzburger points to "covenantal imperatives" extending beyond specific halakhic strictures. In Wurzburger's view, Jewish ethics encompass "not only halakhic rules governing the area of morality, but also intuitive moral responses arising from the covenantal relationship with God."[12] In the words of Tamar Ross, "The ultimate decision as to what Sinaitic Torah means is arrived at by a dialectic between inside and outside forces, with both subsumed under the larger interpretive goal: to achieve a holistic understanding of the divine will."[13]

Donniel Hartman observes of every scripture that it "is never monolithic or completely coherent, and the task of building a religious life entails giving greater weight to certain sections over others."[14] Coherence is constructed through selection and interpretation. This is an important aspect of the vitality of a living Torah.

Jonathan Sacks comments that between creation and the messianic age, there is a long journey to redemption. Jewish time, he avers, "is the supreme narrative of hope," notwithstanding "digression, false turns, wanderings in the wilderness."[15] Visioning the messianic era, Maimonides writes: "In that era, there will be neither famine or war, envy or competition for good will flow in abundance" (*Mishneh Torah*, Laws of Kings 12:5). The Book of Exodus challenges its readers to play an active role in constructing a society that moves toward reflecting that vision.

One aspect of this continuing project is engaging in *tikkun olam*, literally, repairing the world. The Mishnah, compiled circa 200 CE, records that rabbis of earlier generations enacted certain rules for the sake of *tikkun olam*, societal benefit. In the sixteenth century, the term was used in reference to the mystical notion—part of Lurianic Kabbalah—of repairing the cosmos through the performance of *mitzvot*. In the latter part of the twentieth century, the term came to be invoked to describe humanitarian activity more generally. The idea that human actions matter and can, indeed, repair worlds—in whichever sense one understands the phrase—is a call to action.

In his book *The Dignity of Difference*, Jonathan Sacks points out that covenantal relationships are, inherently, pluralistic; one relationship by no means excludes others. No less important is that a covenantal relationship

> reminds us that we are guardians of the past for the sake of the future. It extends our horizons to the chain of the generations of which we are a part. It holds us to the consequences of our actions, from exploitation of the environment to the over-commercialization of society to the utterly unforgivable arms trade and all the other ways in which self-interested conduct in the short term creates hazard in the long term. Covenant means extended responsibility, horizontally across space, vertically across time, to and for the totality of which we are a part.[16]

In his now classic work *Zakhor: Jewish History and Jewish Memory*, Yosef Hayim Yerushalmi notes that "only in Israel and nowhere else is the injunction to remember felt as a religious imperative to an entire people."[17] Jewish memory transmits the past to inform the present and nurture a vision of the future. The covenant of Exodus (Sinai) summons the Jewish people, individually and collectively, to translate the ideals of Torah into action. This evolving project of translation adds meaning to the life of the individual and contributes to advancing the realization of the vision of a world redeemed. It is a project that happens one act at a time.

In a book titled *Civility*, Stephen Carter, a professor at Yale Law School, tells of his experience as an African American child moving with his family to a white neighborhood in the DC area in the 1960s. Sitting outside with his siblings, eleven-year-old Stephen felt ignored and unwelcomed: "I knew we were not welcome here. I knew we would not be liked here. I knew we would have no friends here." Suddenly, a woman returning home from work smiled at the children and, with a broad smile, exclaimed, "Welcome!" She went into her house and soon reappeared bearing a tray laden with drinks and cream cheese and jelly sandwiches for the young Carters. Carter writes that the woman's name was Sara Kestenbaum; Sara was a religious Jew. In Jewish tradition, he continues, such acts of kindness are called *ḥesed*. In that encounter, Carter concludes, "I discovered how a single act of genuine and unassuming civility can change a life forever."[18] Though the covenant of

Exodus is particularistic, the vision it represents and the acts it encourages extend to all humankind. This is the universal dimension of the Jewish covenant; it is a covenant with a universal mission.

Chapter 5

The Book of Leviticus

Ritual and Sanctification; Aspiring to Holiness

The third book of the Torah is known as Leviticus, from the Latin "of the Levites." In Hebrew, the book is called *Vayikra*, "And He called," from the first (Hebrew) word of the book, in which God calls Moses. The book is also known as "*torat kohanim*," instructions for the priests, reflecting the fact that much of its content is directed at the priests of Israel, Aaron and his descendants. Beyond this target audience, the book guides all Israel—commanded to be a "nation of priests" (Exodus 19:6)—toward fulfilling its collective charge.

Leviticus opens with seven chapters devoted to sacrifices that were to be offered individually and collectively by the Israelites. The book proceeds to laws of *kashrut* (dietary laws) and ritual purity. The leitmotif of chapters 17 through 27, often referred to as the Holiness Code, is the Hebrew word *kadosh*, meaning holy, or set apart. Israel is to strive to be holy through its ethical as well as ritual conduct.

The Hebrew word for sacrifice, *korban*, actually derives from the root (*krv*) meaning "near." The ritual of sacrifice was a means of drawing nearer to the Divine. Prior to the paschal offering described in Exodus, chapter 12, the Torah tells of individuals offering animals, on an altar, to God. Such instances, notes theologian Gordon Tucker, are "in times of intense joy, stress or in personal revelatory moments."[1] In the Book of Leviticus, sacrifice is regulated: sacrifices are to be offered at an official altar, and the altar—and hence the sacrificial rite—is controlled by priests.

In addition to the paschal lamb offered by every Israelite household each year, eaten in commemoration of the exodus from Egypt, there are five principal categories of sacrifices: (1) *Olah* (burnt offering), (2) *Minḥah* (grain offering), (3) *Sh'lamim* (sacrifice of well-being), (4) *Ḥattat* (sin offering), and (5) *Asham* (reparation offering). Bible scholar Jacob Milgrom observes that "the rule of thumb for all sacrifices is that the altar is the province of the priest; all other rituals are the province of the offerer."[2]

ON SACRIFICE

Explaining the context of sacrifices to rationalist readers of the twelfth century, Maimonides, in his *Guide for the Perplexed*, points to the principle of "gradual development." Just as in nature change is slow and gradual, "man according to his nature is not capable of abandoning suddenly all to which he was accustomed" (*Guide* 3:32). Sacrifice, Maimonides suggests, was not an ultimate end but part of a process of redirecting the Israelites from idolatry toward a relationship with God. In a recent work on the *Guide for the Perplexed*, Micah Goodman offers the following summary of Maimonides's view:

> When the Jewish people lived as slaves in Egypt . . . the only ways of worship that they knew were offering animals and burning incense. The Torah sought to align itself with people who were receiving it and therefore commanded that they continue offering animals and burning incense, except that now, instead of sacrificing to idols, they were to sacrifice to the God of Israel. Like the martial arts technique of defeating your opponent by turning his own strength against him, the Torah enlisted the power of idolatrous methods in order to overcome idolatry.[3]

Attuned to the gradual pace of spiritual development, the Torah did not proscribe sacrifice but limited and redirected it.

Over the course of centuries, the prophets of Israel reminded the Jewish people that sacrifice was a means to a higher end. Nothing was more detestable to God than wrongful conduct accompanied by sacrificial offerings. A morally corrupt society maintaining ritual practices represents a gross contravention of the Divine Will.

Sacrificial rites properly understood and experienced are to nurture and promote the spirit of priestly holiness that is at the heart of the Book of Leviticus. Commenting on God's "acceptance" of sacrifice (Leviticus 1:4), Nehama Leibowitz notes: "The offering does not, Heaven forfend, itself propitiate the Creator, but serves merely as an expression of man's desire to purify himself and become reconciled with Him."[4] The Mishnah teaches: "It is stated with regard to an animal burnt offering (Lev. 1:9), 'an offering by fire of pleasing odor to the Lord'; with regard to a bird burnt offering (Lev. 1:17), 'an offering by fire of pleasing odor to the Lord'; with regard to a meal offering (Lev. 2:2), 'an offering by fire of pleasing odor to the Lord.' The repetitive language is to say that there is no distinction between one who gives more and one who gives less, provided that the individual's intent is directed to heaven" (Menaḥot 13:11). When it comes to wrongdoings committed against other human beings, the Mishnah famously teaches: "For offenses between man and his Maker Yom Kippur atones; for offenses between man and his neighbor Yom Kippur does not atone until he has appeased his neighbor" (Yoma, 8:9).

If an anointed priest inadvertently sins, he is to bring a purification offering (Leviticus 4:3). The Talmud quotes Yohanan ben Zakkai as having commented: "Fortunate is the generation whose leader recognizes having sinned and brings an offering of purification" (Hor. 10b). Amplifying this teaching, Shai Held observes:

> Like it or not, we learn from our leaders—and so do our children. A generation whose leaders are incapable of apologizing is a generation devoid of a potentially powerful model; a generation whose leaders respond to charges of misconduct by denying, obfuscating, or shifting incessantly to the passive voice ("mistakes were made") is a generation whose children learn to offer an honest, straightforward apology for bad behavior only when their backs are against the wall—only, that is, when all other (self-exonerating) tactics have failed. But a generation whose leaders step forward and say "Yes, I really blew it, and I'm sorry," just might learn the importance of integrity and accountability.[5]

One among the several offerings (in the category of well-being offerings) described in the Book of Leviticus is the thanksgiving offering, the "*korban todah*" (Leviticus 7:12). The Talmud notes that there are four instances when a person should—though the thanksgiving offering is voluntary—offer thanks in this manner: surviving a desert (or other hazardous) journey, imprisonment, serious illness, or a sea voyage (Berakhot 54b). Long after the cessation of sacrifice, the practice of expressing gratitude for having survived dangerous circumstances continues by way of a special blessing (*gomel*) in the Jewish prayer service.

The Book of Exodus closed with construction of the tabernacle and its accoutrements; Leviticus 1–7 turns to sacrifices that are to be offered on the altar. Chapters 8 through 10 tell of the consecration of the priests, the inauguration of the tabernacle service, and the unusual death of two of Aaron's sons. In a dramatic scene, "Aaron lifted his hands toward the people and blessed them; and he stepped down after offering the sin offering, the burnt offering and the offering of well-being" (Leviticus 9:22). The people perceived God's Presence and beheld a fire that "came forth from before the Lord" (Leviticus 9:24), consuming the burnt offering on the altar.

In the very next verse, two of Aaron's sons, Nadab and Abihu, "offered before the Lord alien fire, which He had not enjoined upon them. And fire came forth from the Lord and consumed them" (Leviticus 10:1–2). The episode seems to manifest that religious discipline rather than unbounded ecstasy is expected of the priesthood. In the face of this calamity, Moses says to Aaron that God has conveyed that "through those near to Me I show Myself holy" (Leviticus 10:3). Samson Raphael Hirsch comments, by way of explanation: "the more anybody stands in front of the people as a leader and teacher in relation to Me, the less do I overlook his mistakes."[6]

TOWARD *KEDUSHAH*: HOLINESS

The word *kadosh*, holy, connotes separation. The Torah establishes an ideal that all Israel shall be "a kingdom of priests and a holy (*kadosh*) nation" (Exodus 19:6). "Holiness," Milgrom writes, "is the extension of God's nature; it is the agency of God's will. If certain things are termed holy—such as the land (Canaan), person (priest), place (sanctuary), or time (holy day)—they are so by virtue of divine dispensation."[7]

A life of holiness reflects *imitatio dei*; it is a quest for Godliness. It is worthy of note that the standard "formula" of blessing in Jewish prayer includes the phrase "*asher kiddishanu bemitzvotav*"—Who has sanctified (the Hebrew word is from *kadosh*) us with His command-ments. Performance of a *mitzvah*, the rabbis who authored this declara-tion—and those who recite it—affirm, sanctifies the individual who does it; they become holy by its performance.

Chapter 11 of Leviticus is one of four places in the Torah in which food prohibitions are enumerated. In all four sources, holiness is indi-cated as the reason for the restrictions (Exodus 22:30; Leviticus 11:44–45; Leviticus 20:25–26; Deuteronomy 14:21). Avoidance of "impure" foods contributes to Israel's distinctiveness.

The theme of impurity continues in chapters 12 through 15, with prescriptions relating to ridding oneself of ritual impurity. Summarizing the characteristics of ritual impurity, Jonathan Klawans notes that "(1) The sources of ritual impurity are natural and more or less unavoid-able. (2) It is not sinful to contract these impurities. (3) These impu-rities can convey an impermanent contagion to people (priests and Israelites) and to many items within close proximity."[8] The causes of ritual impurity are contact with human corpses or carcasses of animals, fluxes of life fluids, and a skin condition known as *tzara'at*. "The com-mon denominator," writes Bible scholar Baruch Schwartz, "is that all these are manifestations of death, or more precisely, of the escape of the forces of life."[9] Holiness is the embodiment of life, while impurity represents death.

Noting that childbirth represents both new life and a threat to life, Shai Held comments:

> Maternal ritual impurity is the Torah's way of recognizing the mystery and power of childbirth: A new being has just crossed the boundary into life. But it is also a way of acknowledging the terror that in helping her child across the boundary, the mother faces the risk that she could cross it in the other direction. The risks have been mitigated for many modern women, but they have surely not been eliminated. Leviticus wants us to remain aware of that very stark and sobering fact.[10]

The skin disease termed *tzara'at* is identified by the priest. During the period of a person's affliction with this condition the individual is to dwell outside the camp (Leviticus 13:46). When the *tzara'at* disap-pears, the *kohen* (priest) performs a series of purification rituals and the afflicted individual is reintegrated into the community.

Ritual impurity is simply a fact of life. One who contracts impurity is to attend to its disposal. This is typically accomplished by the passage of a prescribed period of time, cleansing (in water), and a purification offering. Only in a state of ritual purity could a person approach the sanctuary.

Chapter 16 describes the public rituals of Yom Kippur and the responsibilities of the priests for purification of the sanctuary. As part of this process, "Aaron is to offer his own bull of sin offering, to make expiation for himself and for his household" (Leviticus 16:6). The Talmud explains that atonement is not achieved merely by the sacrificial ritual but—in this context and others—must include a verbal confession of sins (Yoma 36b). This confession, S. R. Hirsch comments, is not a confession to another person or, even, to God. It is "an admission to oneself." Hirsch continues, "A genuine 'I have sinned' precludes the recurrence of the sin. Every true self-judgment includes self-knowledge, not only that we should have behaved otherwise, but that we could have behaved otherwise, and by such recognition of our moral freedom of will rejects any excuse for present or future failings."[11] Confession affirms freedom of choice.

Chapter 17 explicitly forbids offering sacrifices anywhere but the tabernacle altar (Leviticus 17:8–9). It is worthy of note that over the past millennium Jews have been murdered because of the accusation of the blood libel, that they kill non-Jewish children and use their blood for ritual purposes. In stark contrast, Leviticus 17 strongly prohibits the consumption of even animal blood: "No person among you shall partake of blood, nor shall the stranger among you partake of blood" (Leviticus 17:10–12).

Chapter 18 opens with the instruction not to copy the practices of the Egyptians and the Canaanites (Leviticus 18:3). Canaan had defiled the land by gross sexual misconduct; *kedushah*, the way of holiness, requires living by a different pattern of conduct (Leviticus 18:24–30). Jacob Milgrom observes that, in the Torah, "ritual purity is always subject to purification, but no ritual remedy exists for moral impurity." Should the entire Israelite community become guilty of moral impurity, "the irrevocable result is the pollution of the land" (Leviticus 18:25; Numbers 34:3–34) "and the exile of its inhabitants" (Leviticus 18:28; 26:14–38).[12]

Leviticus 18:5 pronounces, "You shall keep My laws and My rules, by the pursuit of which man shall live: I am the Lord." The Talmud, focusing on the words "shall live," explains that the laws of the Torah are to be set aside when preservation of life is at stake but for the limited cases of idolatry, forbidden sexual relations, and murder (Sanhedrin 74a). God's laws are understood as life giving, setting the people Israel on the path of holiness.

YOU SHALL BE HOLY FOR I THE LORD YOUR GOD AM HOLY

Chapter 19 of Leviticus opens with the instruction (to Moses): "Speak to the whole Israelite community and say to them: You shall be holy, for I, the Lord your God, am holy" (Leviticus 19:2). The laws that follow are to be communicated in full assembly; they are not for the select few but for the entire congregation of Israel. Nehama Leibowitz notes that, in the laws set forth, "No attempt is made to separate the rulings governing relations between man and his neighbor from those pertaining to man and his Maker . . . both lead to the ultimate aim of holiness."[13]

Drawing from the text of chapter 19, Jacob Milgrom summarizes its content: "Respect your mother and father. Make one day every week separate from the others and separate it with your rest. When you reap your harvest, always leave a segment for the poor and the lonely. Deal honestly with all those you encounter. Pay people their wages before they go home at night, so they should not want for money or food. Judge others fairly and love your neighbor as yourself. Remember that you were a stranger in the land of Egypt and treat the stranger as a citizen." Commenting that this road to holiness spoke powerfully to the ancient Israelites, Milgrom aptly adds that "the directives speak powerfully to us as we wonder how to make our own lives unique and meaningful."[14]

Among the most well-known admonitions of Leviticus 19 are not to put a stumbling block before the blind (19:14) and to love one's fellow as oneself (19:18). Rashi explains that reference to a blind person is to someone "blind to the matter"—that is, the prohibition is not only against placing a stone in the path of someone who is visually impaired but causing harm to someone who is ignorant of a particular situation.

Most commentators interpret Leviticus 19:18 as instructing that one should desire for one's fellow what one would want for oneself if similarly situated. These two commandments, as many others in the chapter, are punctuated by the declaration "I am God." Caring for others—holding fast to God's attributes—is an act of religious devotion.

Leviticus Rabbah, a collection of rabbinic teachings compiled 1,500 years ago, points to the significance of Leviticus 19. "Rabbi Hiyya taught: 'This section was read in an assembly. Why was it read in an assembly? Because most of the Torah's essential principles can be derived from it.' Rabbi Levi said: 'Because the Ten Commandments are included in it'" (Leviticus Rabbah 24:5).

Noting that *mitzvot* relating to interpersonal relations and laws relating to service of God are intertwined throughout this chapter, Hirsch comments: "On the basis of a true Jewish life, social life and so-called religious life form no contrast to each other. . . . Jewish truth teaches: the movement towards God includes the movement towards His human beings."[15] The ritual and the ethical dimensions of Jewish living comprise an organic whole, constituting the path of holiness.

At the close of several chapters setting forth details of conduct that lead toward the goal of holiness, Leviticus calls for avoidance of the obverse of holiness: profaning the name of God. "You shall faithfully observe My commandments: I am the Lord. You shall not profane My holy name, that I may be sanctified" (Leviticus 22:31–32). One who acts in accordance with God's ways brings honor to God and God's Torah; one who brings dishonor to the Torah profanes God's name.

The Talmud observes: "When a man who studies Scriptures and the Oral Law and ministers to Torah scholars doesn't speak nicely to people and his transactions in the marketplace are unpleasant, and he doesn't conduct himself in a trustworthy manner, what do people say about him? 'Woe to so and so who studies the Torah. Woe to his father who taught him Torah. Happy are the people who have not studied Torah. Have you seen so and so who studied Torah; how ugly are his deeds, how broken are his ways'" (Yoma 86a). Such behavior, the Talmud avers, is a profanation of God's holy name.

The Jerusalem Talmud relates that Shimon ben Shetah, a scholar who lived during the second century BCE, purchased a donkey from an Ishmaelite (someone who was not Jewish). The owner had inadvertently left a precious stone under the saddle. When Shimon insisted on returning this treasure, the Ishmaelite exclaimed: "Blessed is the God of Shimon ben Shetah" (Jerusalem Talmud, Bava Metzia 2:5). Right conduct—the path of holiness—sanctifies God's name. *Kiddush HaShem,* sanctification of God—a phrase often used in reference to martyrdom—can find significant expression in "ordinary" acts of daily life.

Chapter 23 of Leviticus sets forth a calendar of festivals marking holiness in time. It is a list that also appears in Exodus 34, Numbers 28–29, and Deuteronomy 16, in each case with varying emphases. Israel's responsibility for observing the holiday calendar and bringing prescribed offerings is followed, in chapter 24, with the responsibility of supplying daily oil for the tabernacle lamps and weekly bread for the tabernacle table.

THE JUBILEE YEAR, TERMS OF THE COVENANT, CONSECRATION

Chapter 25 opens with the Sabbatical year: "Six years you may sow your field and six years you may prune your vineyard and gather in the yield. But in the seventh year the land shall have a Sabbath of complete rest, a sabbath of the Lord: you shall not sow your field or prune your vineyard" (Leviticus 25:3–4). The Torah then turns to the Jubilee year: "And you shall hallow the fiftieth year. You shall proclaim release throughout the land for all its inhabitants" (Leviticus 25:10). During the Jubilee year, families are to reclaim the land they originally owned and slaves (bound by indentured servitude) are to be freed. Selling land is, in effect, leasing it until the Jubilee year.

Commentators have noted that release (liberty) is proclaimed to *all* the land's inhabitants. Those who as debtors had been enslaved were released and recovered land. Those already in possession of land are among the liberated when all are free. Israel is to remember that it is God who owns the land; all Israelites are God's tenants (Leviticus 25:23).

The Torah prescribes a path to mitigating instances of poverty. "If your kinsman, being in straits, comes under your authority . . . let him live by your side. Do not exact from him advance or accrued interest" (Leviticus 25:35–36). Rashi comments that one should not wait for someone to falter to the point where it will be hard for him to recover; rather, one should strengthen him the moment his means decline. Rashi offers the following analogy: To what may this be compared? To a burden on the ass's back. While it is on the ass, one man can get hold of it and right it, but once it has fallen to the ground, five men cannot lift it.

Chapter 26 presents a series of blessings juxtaposed against a series of curses; each depends on Israel's conduct. Verses 3 through 13 assure that God's blessings will abound if Israel is faithful to the terms of the covenant, pursuing the way of holiness. Verses 14 through 39 describe the severe consequences—including exile from the land—of Israel's failure to fulfill its covenantal obligations. Yet in such an eventuality, if Israel confesses its iniquity, "I will remember in their favor the covenant with the ancients, whom I freed from the land of Egypt in the sight of the nations to be their God: I, the Lord" (Leviticus 26:45).

The Book of Leviticus closes with a chapter on the consecration of resources to support the sanctuary. As with sacrificial offerings and the many practices leading toward a life of *kedushah*, the sanctuary represented a route to experiencing a sense of God's presence. Contributing to its maintenance helped ensure this path toward realizing the holiness that is at the heart of *Vayikra*.

Chapter 6

The (Many) Ways of Sanctification

Some years ago, I met with a group of Israeli teachers whose schools in Tel Aviv were twinned with a variety of Jewish day schools in Los Angeles. The twinning involved shared curricular units and faculty and student exchanges. In this case, Israeli educators had spent a week at the school with which their school was twinned, augmented by a bit of sightseeing and Shabbat meals at the homes of families from their local school "twin." I asked the educators if they would share something that made a particularly significant impression on them, a takeaway with which they would return to Israel.

Among the visiting teachers was a young man with a shaved head, wearing an earring in one ear. I was not surprised to learn that he taught in a secular Israeli public school. His response to my question was the following: "I am the parent of two young children. On Friday night, I was at the home of a family and saw the parents bless their children. I had never seen this before, and it touched me very deeply. This is a beautiful ritual that I plan to initiate in my home, each week, when I'm back in Tel Aviv."

You might recall that, in blessing Ephraim and Manasseh, Joseph's sons, Jacob said that, by their names, future generations would be blessed. It is a custom in many Jewish households for parents to bless their sons that they be like Ephraim and Manasseh and their daughters that they be like Sarah, Rebecca, Rachel, and Leah, the matriarchs of Israel. These declarations are followed by the threefold blessing that was, in keeping with the Torah's instruction, pronounced by the priests (the priestly blessing—the oldest, extant, segment of Torah text discovered to date—also remains part of synagogue liturgy). As with this simple but powerful "at home" Friday night ritual, "Jewish ritual," writes Daniel Gordis, "is about interrupting the pace of modern life to provide a chance to think about and to celebrate that which is more enduring, more compelling, and more important."[1]

Many chapters of Leviticus deal, specifically, with rituals of sacrifice. The same book emphasizes holiness in action toward others as God's instruction to the people Israel. As set forth in the Torah, holiness is not only a matter of ritual practice, it is also expressed in interpersonal relationships and creating a society built on justice and compassion.

To perform ritual acts while not striving for sanctification through right conduct is an abomination. Thus, for example, the prophet Isaiah declares, in God's name: "'What need have I of all your sacrifices?' Says the Lord. 'I am sated with burnt offerings of rams, And suet of fatlings, And blood of bulls; And I have no delight In lambs and he-goats. That you come to appear before Me—Who asked that of you? Trample My courts no more; Bringing oblations is futile, Incense is offensive to Me. New moon and sabbath, Proclaiming of solemnities, Assemblies with iniquity, I cannot abide. Your new moons and fixed seasons Fill Me with loathing; They are become a burden to Me, I cannot endure them'" (Isaiah 1:11–14).

Rituals are neither mechanical nor magical acts. They are or, ideally, become suffused with meaning for the one who engages in the action. Over the centuries, Jewish thinkers have explored *ta'amei ha-mitzvot*, the rationales for the broad array of *mitzvot* of the Torah; there is a body of literature on this subject, as Jews in various times and places probed the meaning of the Torah's action-instructions. Engaging in the action often leads to appreciation and understanding of its significance.

For nearly two thousand years, prayer has supplanted sacrifice as a vehicle for arriving at the nearness to God that was the aim of sacrificial offerings. Abraham Joshua Heschel points to the pedagogic dimension of prayer: "Prayer teaches us what to aspire to. So often we do not know what to cling to. Prayer implants in us the ideals we ought to cherish. Redemption, purity of mind and tongue or willingness to help, may hover as ideas before our mind, but the idea becomes a concern, something to long for, a goal to be reached, when we pray."[2] Prayers of praise emerge, writes Heschel, through "wonder and radical amazement," expressing a "sense of God's majesty and glory."[3]

Discussing when in the morning it is light enough to recite *sh'ma yisrael*, the declaration that God is One, the Talmud indicates that an individual can first engage in this liturgical act *misheyakir et ḥavero*, from when it is light enough that one can recognize an acquaintance of average familiarity from a distance of about six feet (Berakhot 9b). That an individual is moved to relate to God upon arising in the morning is commendable. One must first, however, recognize other human beings, fellow travelers in the journey of life, who are created in God's image.

For Mordecai Kaplan, who understood God as "the force that makes for salvation"—that is, the power in nature that actualizes potential for good—prayer serves to connect the individual with the power that motivates and actualizes that potential. For Kaplan, *mitzvot* are *sancta*, spiritual symbols that fortify the collective conscience of the Jewish people. Rather than "commandments," ritual *mitzvot*, in his view, are in the nature of *minhagim*, folkways that characterize Jewish civilization.

The Hebrew verb "to pray," *l'hitpalel*, means to judge oneself. There is an aspect of self-judgment in prayer, reflecting on one's actions in the light of articulated values. As with the array of sacrifices, there are various sorts of prayers including thanksgiving, praise, petition, acknowledgment of wrongdoing, and aspirations. The Jewish prayer book, called *siddur*, is the order of the liturgy.

Heschel notes that there is a tension between *keva*, the fixed structure of prayer, and *kavanah*, inner devotion, and a need to achieve equilibrium between the two. "Jewish prayer," Heschel explains, "is guided by two opposite principles: order and outburst, regularity and spontaneity, uniformity and individuality, law and freedom, a duty and a prerogative, empathy and self-expression, insight and sensitivity, creed and faith, the word and that which is beyond words." He adds that "it [this polarity] . . . concerns not only prayer but the whole sphere of Jewish observance."[4]

There are three daily prayer services, morning, afternoon, and night, and blessings for experiences of enjoyment, for the privilege of performing various *mitzvot*, and blessings of thanksgiving, petition, or praise. There are prayers on awakening in the morning and when going to sleep at night. One of my teachers, Ḥazzan (Cantor) Binyamin Glickman, shared with me the following understanding of the prayer recited by many Jews immediately upon awakening: "*Modeh ani*: I thank You, Living and eternal King, for giving me back my soul in mercy. Your faith (in me) is great."[5] Understood in this way, the statement recognizes the responsibility that devolves on the individual as God's trusted partner; it is a powerful orientation to the new day.

In like manner, Samson Raphael Hirsch notes that the typical "formula" of blessing, *Barukh atah*, blessed be You, is not about God's blessing the individual. "The Jew, in effect, is saying: You have entrusted the fulfillment of Your will, the granting of Your wishes, the promotion of Your Kingdom, the implementation of Your work, to man's free will. It is for this purpose that I am, that I exist." The declarant is saying, "may God be blessed through me."[6]

The Book of Leviticus directs all Israel to be holy. The Jew is to strive to be holy, and the Torah's guidance for pursuit of holiness is pervasive in the sense of relating to every dimension of life. Yitz Greenberg writes: "Judaism is the Jewish way to get humanity from the world as it is now to the world of final perfection. To get from here to there, you need both the goal and a process to keep you going over the long haul of history."[7] The performance of *mitzvot* is an expression of covenantal living and the pursuit of holiness.

As earlier noted, successive generations of Jews have interpreted the Torah informed by its ethos and values and the evolution of ideas in the world of which they are part. In the twenty-first century, considerable interpretive attention has focused on Leviticus 18 and the prohibition of homosexuality, described as *toeivah*, an abhorrent act. While the Torah (only) explicitly references male homosexual relations (Lev. 18:22), early rabbinic texts and later codes forbade lesbian relations as well.

On the backdrop of contemporary understanding of homosexuality, *responsa* (rabbinic opinions grounded in Jewish sources) have revisited the biblical text, suggesting a much more narrow, limited meaning of the prohibition than has hitherto been heard. For example, writing of a relationship between two women who "seek to build a Jewish home together with love and commitment," Rabbi Jeffrey Fox, Rosh HaYeshiva, Yeshivat Maharat, writes that not only ought the relationship not be deemed *prizuta* (licentiousness), rather, "this should be understood as *tzniuta* (modesty) and perhaps even *kedushata* (holiness)."[8] As Tamar Ross observes, Torah remains "the rock-bottom cultural linguistic filter through which new 'hearings' are understood," although "changing circumstances appear to turn the import of the original message . . . on its head."[9]

While neither ignoring nor reinterpreting the language of Leviticus 18:22, Orthodox rabbis have emphasized the imperative of respect for all people, recognizing that each individual is created *betzelem Elohim*, in the image of God. In this spirit, Rabbi Ephraim Mirvis, chief rabbi of the United Hebrew Congregations of Great Britain and the Commonwealth, published a Guide for Orthodox Schools focused on the well-being of LGBT+ students. In it, he affirms: "We are, of course, aware of the Torah's *issurim* (prohibitions) here, including *Vayikra*/Leviticus 18:22, but when homophobic, biphobic and transphobic bullying is carried out with 'justifications' from Jewish texts, a major *chilul Hashem* (desecration of God's name) is caused. We must be ever-mindful of the *mitzvah* to 'Love your neighbor as yourself' (*Vayikra*/Leviticus 19:18), considered by Rabbi Akiva to be the most important principle of the Torah."[10]

Noting that "within our Jewish communities, it is our responsibility to make everyone feel valued," he points out that "there are many Jewish values, expressed through good *middot* (character traits) which apply equally to our conduct regarding each and every one of us, such as *ahavat yisrael* (love of a fellow Jew), the *pintele yid* (the spark of holiness in all of us) and the *tzelem Elohim* (the image of God in which we are all created). No-one should be hurt by breaches of *shmirat halashon* (careless speech) or excluded through lack of *kavod habriyot* (respect for all people)."[11] More liberal streams of Judaism have been yet more embracing of the variety of sexual identities and relationships, beyond affirming the dignity of each individual.[12] This is but one example of a topic of lively, "real-time" conversation regarding the application of Torah to contemporary life.

Though it is not the only book of the Torah that presents the annual calendar of Torah-described holidays, Leviticus devotes an entire chapter (chapter 23) to the cycle of festivals. Jewish holidays are part of the project of becoming holy. Shabbat, occurring every seventh day, celebrates both creation and freedom from slavery. As Heschel describes it, "The seventh day is the armistice in man's cruel struggle for existence, a truce in all conflicts, personal and social, peace between man and man, man and nature, peace within man." He comments: "In the tempestuous ocean of time and toil there are islands of stillness where man may enter a harbor and reclaim his dignity. The island is the seventh day, the Sabbath, a day of detachment from things, instruments and practical affairs as well as of attachment to the spirit."[13] Shabbat is, in short, holiness in time. Particularly in a technological age, when one can feel quite "on call," 24/7, the act of "unplugging" for twenty-five hours each week, creating a sanctuary in time, represents a powerful expression of freedom.

The calendar cycle in Leviticus, chapter 23, next turns to Passover, the holiday of Israel's liberation from Egypt. Many of the details of the holiday's observance are by way of reenactment. While the paschal offering is ancient history, the Passover seder shares a story and communicates values across the generations. As Yitz Greenberg writes, "it turns memory into moral dynamic."[14]

Shavuot, literally "weeks," is a harvest holiday, as presented in the Torah. There is a seven-week count from the first day after the start of Passover, leading from the spring holiday (Pesaḥ) to the holiday of the summer harvest. Over time, Shavuot came to be associated with the Israelites' experience at Sinai. The holiday connects celebration of freedom from bondage to embracing a covenant at Sinai, fifty days later.

In the seventh month of the Hebrew calendar year (the first month, in the Torah, is reckoned as the spring month of the Exodus) there is a holiday of remembrance and sounding of the shofar. This holiday, which became known as Rosh HaShanah (head of the year), was, in time, associated with the creation of the world (as distinguished from the first month in the national life of the Israelites, that is, the month of leaving Egypt). The holiday of shofar blasts is a prelude to Yom Kippur, the Day of Atonement, observed on the tenth day of the seventh month. The ten-day period that opens this month (the Hebrew month known as Tishrei) is one of introspection and return (Hebrew: *teshuvah*) to the path of covenantal living.

The closing, Torah-prescribed festivals are the holiday of Sukkot and an eighth day of convocation following the seven-day Sukkot holiday. Sukkot is both a fall harvest festival and a commemoration of dwelling in temporary booths during years of desert wandering. The celebration known as Shemini Atzeret, the Eighth Day of Assembly, is a festival day not unlike Sukkot but without any of the rituals (the sukkah or four species) unique to that holiday. Over the course of time, Simḥat Torah—marking the close of the year-long cycle of Torah study as part of the synagogue service and resuming it anew—was attached to Shemini Atzeret, the eighth day. In Israel and in those communities that celebrate the holidays based on the number of days stipulated in the Torah, Shemini Atzeret and Simḥat Torah are celebrated on the same day. In those communities outside Israel that celebrate an "extra" day of the Torah-prescribed holidays, Simḥat Torah is celebrated as the second day of Shemini Atzeret.

Reflecting on the holiday calendar, Yitz Greenberg comments that "the calendar constantly shapes and deepens group memory." During the course of the year, "every Jew lives through all of Jewish history and makes it his or her personal experience. Through the power of the calendar and the community, each individual life is linked to a cause that transcends it."[15]

Beyond the period of the Torah, additional holidays entered the Jewish calendar cycle, starting with Purim and Hanukkah. Further commemorations, both celebratory and memorial in nature, have become part of the Jewish calendar, a demonstration of the continuing vitality of a living tradition.[16] Among the most recent additions to the calendar in Israel and among many Jews in other lands are Yom HaShoah (Holocaust Memorial Day), Yom HaZikaron (Israel's Memorial Day), and Yom HaAtzmaut (Israel's Day of Independence). The holidays are milestones for the individual and occasions for community reflection or celebration. The place of community in Jewish life is a central theme in the Book of Numbers to which we next turn.

Chapter 7

The Book of Numbers

Living in Community

The Book of Numbers, known in Hebrew as *Bamidbar* ("in the wilderness"), tells of more than thirty-eight years of the forty-year period of the Torah's narrative of the journey of the Israelites from Egypt to the edge of the Promised Land. It opens with a census (hence, the name Numbers) in preparation for the journey from the wilderness of Sinai toward Canaan. It includes a second census decades later, as the generation of those born in freedom prepares for the conquest and settlement of the land. Throughout the book, the tribes of Israel must learn to live in community. Those who left Egypt fall far short of the ideals to which the Israelites are summoned at Sinai and in the holiness code of Leviticus.

THE WILDERNESS CAMP

Chapters 1 through 10 of Numbers are set during the opening months of the second year from the time of the exodus from Egypt. The Israelites are instructed to camp "each with his standard, under the banners of their ancestral house; they shall camp around the Tent of Meeting at a distance" (Numbers 2:2). The tabernacle, with the ark as its centerpiece, was central to the collective identity of the Israelites. The Levites are charged with special responsibility for protection of the sanctuary.

In preparation for the wilderness journey, the Israelites are reminded of the need to maintain the purity of the camp. Those who experienced various ritual impurities—skin diseases, genital discharges, or contact

with a corpse—required temporary removal from the camp and a purification ritual. This, the text conveys, would avoid defilement of the
camp (Numbers 5:3).

The chapter that begins with instances of ritual impurity ends with
the case of a suspected adulteress. As with purification from ritual
impurity, it is the priest who is to address the situation, orchestrating a
process (described in Numbers 5:11–31) designed to resolve the question of whether the husband's suspicion is warranted. Jacob Milgrom
observes that "jurisdiction in this case lies outside the human court."
The prescribed procedure removes jurisdiction and punishment from
human hands, guaranteeing that the accused "would not be put to
death."[1] Based on a verse that says that "the man shall be clear of guilt"
(Numbers 5:31), Samson Raphael Hirsch comments that the husband
can only expect a decision if "he knows himself to be free from the
same sexual misbehavior, yea, from every sexual misbehavior."[2]

THE NAZIRITE, THE PRIESTLY BLESSINGS

Chapter 6 opens by describing the status of a Nazirite, a man or woman
who consecrates himself or herself to God for a limited period of time,
becoming a sort of lay priest. The Nazirite takes on such restrictions as
abstaining from fermented drinks and grape products, abstaining from
cutting his or her hair, and abstaining from any contact with the dead.
At the close of the stipulated period, a Nazirite would undergo ritual
immersion and bring a variety of offerings, through the priest.

While explanations of the rationales for these offerings vary, it might
be that the *hattat* (sin) offering is atonement for withdrawing from the
world, a withdrawal that is not viewed as a religious ideal. An *olah*
(burnt offering) serves as expiation for the nazir's having, perhaps, considered himself to be exalted, "above" the community. Finally, a peace
offering demonstrates the nazir's reintegration into the community.

Among the duties of the priests was blessing the community of Israel
in the name of the Lord. The threefold blessing "The Lord bless you and
protect you! The Lord deal kindly and graciously with you! The Lord
bestow His favor upon you and grant you peace!" (Numbers 6:24–26)
is, in Hebrew, an escalating sequence of three, five, and seven words.
Nehama Leibowitz notes that this crescendo begins with material needs,

proceeds to spiritual matters, and rises to a crowning climax of the blessing of peace.[3] Amulets bearing inscriptions of these blessings have been unearthed outside ancient Jerusalem, dating to the seventh or sixth century BCE.[4]

CONSECRATING THE TABERNACLE

Chapter 7 turns to the sacrifices brought by each of the tribal chieftains at the consecration of the tabernacle. Each one brought precisely the same offering, but each is separately detailed (Numbers 7:1–88). Nehama Leibowitz suggests that "perhaps the Torah wished to emphasize the importance and uniqueness of the individual, repudiating the ideology that regards the human being as a cog in a vast machine and as an indistinguishable member of a mass."[5]

Shai Held amplifies this thought, affirming that "being part of a collective, no matter how important or sacred, should never be allowed—must never be allowed—to obliterate human difference and individuality."[6] Held continues, "I would suggest that a Jewish community worthy of the name is thus charged to honor two facts simultaneously: As Jews and as human beings, we share deep connection and kinship, and at the same time we are irreducibly different from one another. To live together is to nurture what connects us even as we affirm and celebrate what renders us unique."[7]

FINAL PREPARATION FOR THE JOURNEY

Following instructions for lighting the menorah and guidance for purification of the Levites (chapter 8), the Torah turns to observance of the second Passover, trumpet signals for assembling and for breaking camp, and the order of the march (chapters 9 and 10). Guided by a cloud, Israel leaves Sinai, heading toward the wilderness of Paran. As the Israelites march, they maintain an established order of divisions, tribes, and clans, with the ark and tabernacle accompanying them. No sooner does the journey resume than "the people took to complaining" (Numbers 11:1), a motif that will recur through much of the ensuing narrative of *Bamidbar*.

CRAVING, COMPLAINTS, AND RESPONSE

In like fashion to complaints heard soon after the exodus from Egypt, the Torah describes the people's craving and nostalgia surrounding the good food they had eaten in Egypt: "We remember the fish that we used to eat free in Egypt, the cucumbers, the melons, the leeks, the onions, and the garlic" (Numbers 11:5). They clamor, too, for meat.

Moses exclaims to God, "I cannot carry all this people by myself, for it is too much for me" (Numbers 11:14). God instructs Moses to gather seventy of Israel's elders. "I will draw upon the spirit that is on you and put it upon them; they shall share the burden of the people with you, and you shall not bear it alone" (Numbers 11:17). Moses does as instructed, and "the spirit rested upon them" (Numbers 11:25).

The Torah proceeds to tell of two men, Eldad and Medad, who—after the elders have, apparently, dispersed—begin to speak in ecstasy. Joshua, Moses's attendant, urges Moses to restrain them. Moses responds, "Are you wrought up on my account? Would that all the Lord's people were prophets, that the Lord put His spirit upon them!" (Numbers 11:29).

Samson Raphael Hirsch comments: "Moses's answer to Joshua remains for all teachers and leaders as the brilliant example they should keep before their eyes as the highest ideal aim of their work, viz., to make themselves superfluous, and the people of all classes and ranks reach such a spiritual level that they no longer require teachers and leaders."[8] As contemporary theologian Shai Held observes: "Leaders who needily pursue their own glory and institutions that focus on their own self-perpetuation—sometimes even at the expense of the very values they purport to uphold—are sadly prevalent in our world. In the face of all that stands Moses, the paradigmatic leader who internalizes the simple but profound truth: It's not about you."[9]

As to satisfying the people's craving for meat, God's *ruaḥ* (in Hebrew, *ruaḥ* means both spirit and wind) brings an abundance of quail. With the meat still between their teeth (Numbers 11:33), the people are struck by a plague. The place is, accordingly, named *kivrot ha-ta'avah*, graves of craving.

MIRIAM, AARON, AND MOSES: DISCORD AND RECONCILIATION

Chapter 12 relates an instance of tension between Moses and his siblings. They (Aaron and Miriam) said: "Has the Lord spoken only through Moses? Has He not spoken through us as well?" (Numbers 12:2). God communicates that the standing of Moses is unique: "How then did you not shrink from speaking against My servant Moses!" (Numbers 12:8). Miriam, who seems to have initiated the critique of Moses (Numbers 12:1), is stricken with skin disease.

Aaron calls on Moses to pray on their sister's behalf. Moses responds with a five-word prayer: "O God, pray heal her" (Numbers 12:13). Miriam, healed of her snow white scales, is subjected to a seven-day exclusion from the camp. When she is readmitted, the Israelites proceed with their journey, encamping in the wilderness of Paran.

THE RECONNAISSANCE OF CANAAN: A JOURNEY OF FORTY YEARS

Chapter 13 turns to the dispatch of twelve scouts—leaders of the Israelite tribes—to bring report of the land of Canaan. Moses's charge to them is: "See what kind of country it is. Are the people who dwell in it strong or weak, few or many? Is the country in which they dwell good or bad? Are the towns they live in open or fortified? Is the soil rich or poor? Is it wooded or not?" (Numbers 13:18–20).

The scouts go forth and return, reporting that the land "does indeed flow with milk and honey. . . . However, the people who inhabit the country are powerful, and the cities are fortified" (Numbers 13:27–28). The Hebrew word for "however," *efes*, also the word for zero, connotes impossibility. In addition to describing the land—their stated mission—the scouts convey the view that conquest of Canaan is beyond the Israelites' power.

Caleb, one of the delegation of twelve, challenges the majority conclusion. He declares: "Let us by all means go up, and we shall gain possession of it (the land), for we shall surely overcome it" (Numbers 13:30). All but Joshua, among the scouts, reply: "it (the people of the land) is stronger than we" (Numbers 13:31).

Expanding on their assessment of relative strength, the scouts pronounce that "we looked like grasshoppers to ourselves, and so we must have looked to them" (Numbers 13:33). There is no apparent basis for the scouts' knowing how the inhabitants of the land viewed them. Seeing themselves as grasshoppers, they concluded, though, that this must be their image in the eyes of others.

The response of the Israelite community was loud cries and weeping. "And they said to one another, 'Let us head back for Egypt'" (Numbers 14:4). The insecurity of freedom was, for the generation that had known slavery from birth, overwhelming: better to be governed, even as slaves, by others. As Nehama Leibowitz describes it, "they spurned the opportunity to lead their own lives, foster their own economy and govern themselves."[10] The scouts could not see positive possibilities; they saw only insurmountable challenges. On this backdrop, it is only the generation of Israelites born in freedom, save Caleb and Joshua, who will, after forty years, enter the promised land (Numbers 14:26–38).

Chapter 15 of *Bamidbar* sets forth a variety of laws, many of which are to be observed upon entering the land of Israel. Though the generation that left Egypt will die in the desert, the promised future will be realized by their children. The chapter closes, however, with a law that could, immediately, be observed: "Speak to the Israelite people and instruct them to make for themselves fringes on the corners of their garments throughout the ages" (Numbers 15:38). This *mitzvah* of *tzitzit* (fringes) is so "you shall be reminded to observe all My commandments and to be holy to your God" (Numbers 15:40). Wearing *tzitzit*, the Torah conveys, is a tangible reminder of the summons to be holy, the fundamental call to the Jewish people.

THE KORAH REBELLION AND ITS AFTERMATH

Chapter 16 opens with a challenge to the leadership of Moses and Aaron. Korah (a Levite), joined by Dathan and Abiram, On, and 250 princes from among the Israelites, declares: "all the community are holy, all of them, and the Lord is in their midst. Why then do you raise yourselves above the Lord's congregation?" (Numbers 16:3). United in opposing Moses and Aaron, the rebel faction, in typical demagogic fashion, invokes the holy status of the community—which it presumes to represent—with no positive platform.

Commenting on the alliance of the named leaders of the rebellion, Rashi takes note of the arrangement of the tribes as they traveled in the desert. The family of Korah encamped near the tribe of Reuben, from which Korah apparently enlisted Dathan and Abiram as coconspirators. Quoting a midrash, Rashi observes: "Woe to the evildoer and woe to his neighbor."

The Mishnah (Avot 5:20) famously teaches that "every controversy that is in the name of heaven shall in the end lead to a permanent result; but every controversy that is not in the name of heaven shall not lead to a permanent result. Which controversy was that which was in the name of heaven? Such was the controversy of Hillel and Shammai. And that which was not in the name of heaven? Such was the controversy of Korah and all his company."

Nehama Lebowitz quotes Malbim (acronym for Meir Leibush ben Yehiel Michel, 1809–1879), who explains the distinction between controversies pursued in the name of heaven and those not pursued for this cause in the following terms: "In a holy or heavenly cause both sides are, in fact, united by one purpose, to further unselfish, Divine ends. However, in a controversy pursued for unholy ends, for personal advancement and the like even those who have come together on one side are not really united. Each are governed by their own calculations of what they stand to gain and are ready to cut each other's throats if it so serves their interests."[11]

In the case of Korah, Malbim suggests that Korah sought the High Priesthood. Dathan, Abiram, and On, of the tribe of Jacob's first-born son (Reuben), thought that they were entitled to high office. The 250 Israelite "princes of the community" resented that a hereditary priesthood had been established rather than their appointment to that role. While sacred and altruistic motives were put forward in challenging the leadership of Moses and Aaron, self-aggrandizement stood at the heart of the rebellion. The Korah insurrection ends, as "the earth opened its mouth and swallowed them up with their households, all Korah's people and all their possessions" (Numbers 16:32).

In chapter 17, the special roles of the tribe of Levi for sanctuary duties and of Aaron and his family as priests are reconfirmed. The ensuing chapter sets forth a system for compensating the priests and Levites

for their services. Prior to resuming the narrative of the Israelites' journey, the Torah presents (Numbers 19) the ritual of the red cow, a means
of purifying individuals in the event of ritual contamination through
contact with a corpse.

THE DEATH OF MIRIAM;
PUNISHMENT OF MOSES AND AARON

The Israelites proceed to Kadesh; the Torah reports: "Miriam died there
and was buried there" (Numbers 20:1). The text immediately turns to
a new, though previously encountered, complaint of the Israelites: the
lack of water to drink (Numbers 20:4–5). Moses is instructed: "You
and your brother Aaron take the rod and assemble the community, and
before their very eyes order the rock to yield its water. Thus you shall
produce water for them from the rock and provide drink for the congregation and their beasts" (Numbers 20:8).

Moses takes the rod but, on assembling the people, says to them,
"'Listen, you rebels, shall we get water for you out of this rock?' And
Moses raised his hand and struck the rock twice with his rod. Out came
copious water, and the community and their beasts drank" (Numbers
20:10–11).

Though abundant water issues forth, Moses and Aaron have failed
in their leadership. The text relates that "the Lord said to Moses and
Aaron, 'Because you did not trust Me enough to affirm My sanctity in
the sight of the Israelite people, therefore you shall not lead this congregation into the land that I have given them'" (Numbers 20:12). Many
interpretations have been offered by way of explaining the wrongdoing
of Moses and Aaron.

Three of the classical biblical commentators of the eleventh, twelfth,
and thirteenth centuries offer three different perspectives. Rashi (1040–
1105) suggests that striking rather than speaking to the rock diminished
the people's perception of the miraculous nature of the occurrence.
Maimonides (1135–1204) points to the anger expressed in Moses's
pronouncement: "Listen you rebels." This anger was not only unbecom-
ing a leader, it might have also conveyed a sense that God is angry and
wrathful. Nahmanides (1194–1270) focuses on the question "shall we
get water for you," observing that the words seem to arrogate to Moses

and Aaron the production of water from the rock. Whichever explanation one prefers, the episode conveys that, after forty years, Moses is frustrated and emotionally frayed; new leadership is needed.

THE JOURNEY CONTINUES;
THE DEATH OF AARON

From Kadesh, where the Israelites were encamped, Moses sends messengers to the King of Edom looking to cross Edomite territory. The request is rebuffed. Soon thereafter, Moses and Eleazar, Aaron's son, accompany Aaron to Mount Hor. There Aaron transfers the priestly vestments to Eleazar. Aaron ascends to the summit of the mountain where he dies. The Israelites mourn the death of Aaron for thirty days before proceeding on the journey.

The Israelites march through Transjordan. Eventually, they encounter Sihon, King of the Amorites. Sihon gathers his troops and engages in battle, "But Israel put them to the sword, and took possession of their land, from the Arnon to the Jabbok" (Numbers 21:24). Israel next engages with King Og of Bashan and, again, emerges victorious (Numbers 21:33–35).

ENCOUNTERING THE MOABITES:
BALAK AND BALAAM

The King of Moab, Balak, having seen others fall before the advancing Israelites, sends messengers to summon a well-known sorcerer endowed with prophecy, Balaam, to curse the approaching Israelites. While initially declining to get involved, Balaam eventually responds to the king's invitation. Recognizing his powers as a Divine gift, Balaam represents to Balak that, though well aware of the desired outcome of his commission, "I can utter only the word that God puts into my mouth" (Numbers 22:38).

Three times, from three different locations, Balaam, after elaborate preparations, overlooks the camp of Israel and utters words of blessings. A verse from one of his blessings has become part of the liturgy: "how fair are your tents, O Jacob, your dwellings, O Israel" (Numbers 24:5).

Balak angrily declares: "I called you to damn my enemies, and instead you have blessed them these three times!" (Numbers 24:10).

The Torah makes clear that the gifts with which people are endowed can either be well used or abused. In the words of Nehama Leibowitz: "Man's natural qualities do not determine his spiritual status, nor do the talents bestowed on him from above." Rather, "man's own will is the sole factor determining whether he will use his qualities, talents and even the gift of prophecy bestowed on him for good, or, God forbid, misuse them, for evil."[12]

THE APOSTASY OF BAAL-PEOR WORSHIP

Following his failed attempts to curse the Israelites, Balaam gives King Balak some information (Numbers 24:14). Rashi explains that his counsel was that the Israelites' downfall could be accomplished through encouraging sexual improprieties. Chapter 25 opens with men of Israel engaging in sexual relations with Moabite women. This leads to sacrifices to and worship of Baal-peor, the cultic god of the Moabites.

When Zimri, a prince of the tribe of Simeon, flagrantly—in sight of the Tent of Meeting—engages in such acts with the daughter of a leader of the Midianites, Phinehas (the son of Eleazar the son of Aaron the priest), stabs the couple, protecting the sanctity of the sanctuary. A plague that claimed thousands of Israelite lives thereupon ceases. Phinehas is granted a covenant of peace. Perhaps the "covenant of peace" stands as a muted rebuke of the behavior of Phinehas. Jacob Milgrom suggests that "God's covenant meant that Phinehas received divine protection against the revenge that would be sought by Zimri's clan."[13]

APPORTIONMENT OF THE LAND:
THE DAUGHTERS OF ZELOPHEHAD

Chapter 26 describes a second census, this time of the generation that will enter the Promised Land. The census of able-bodied men relates to preparation for war as well as apportionment of the land. Plans for the division of the land among the various tribes and households are announced.

The daughters of Zelophehad, women whose father had died, leaving no male offspring, approach Moses, requesting: "Give us a holding among our father's kinsmen!" (Numbers 27:4). The text records: "And the Lord said to Moses, 'The plea of Zelophehad's daughters is just: you should give them a hereditary holding among their father's kinsmen; transfer their father's share to them'" (Numbers 27:6–7). Later, the Torah will stipulate that, in such cases, daughters are to marry within the clan (chapter 36).

LEADERSHIP SUCCESSION

Moses is reminded that, while he will see the land of Israel from a mountaintop, he will not lead the people into the Promised Land. Moses asks God, "the Lord, Source of the breath of all flesh" (Numbers 27:16), to appoint someone over the community so that they will not be like sheep without a shepherd. Rashi, commenting on this verse, accounts for the unusually long description of God as a statement of the following: "Master of the universe, the character of each person is revealed to You, and no two are alike. Appoint over them a leader who will tolerate each person according to his individual character."

Moses is instructed to publicly place his hand upon Joshua (Numbers 27:18), by way of conferring the mantle of leadership. Rashi notes that the biblical text reports that "He [Moses] laid his hands [plural, rather than singular as instructed] upon him" (Numbers 27:23). Rashi explains that Moses, always dedicated to the best interests of the people Israel, did this as an act of generosity, hoping to fully transmit to Joshua the accumulated wisdom that he had acquired over his decades of leadership.

THE CALENDAR OF PUBLIC SACRIFICES
AND FULFILLMENT OF VOWS

Chapters 28 and 29 review the public sacrifices that are to be brought once the people have settled in the land. In addition to the public offerings, personal offerings can also be presented (29:39). As individual sacrifices were sometimes a fulfillment of vows, the Torah next turns to the matter of oaths.

While an oath taken by a man must be fulfilled, a woman's vow can be nullified by her father or husband (if she is married) but only on the day he learns of it. Milgrom comments that "the law reflects the sociological reality that women in biblical days were subservient to their fathers or husbands."[14] If her father or husband does not object on the day he learns of the vow, the oath is valid; if the woman is forced by male authority to break it, the responsibility for nonfulfillment devolves on the man.

THE WAR AGAINST MIDIAN AND SETTLEMENT OF TRANSJORDAN

Chapter 31 recounts a victory over the Midianites without a single Israelite casualty. The tribes of Reuben and Gad, seeing the conquered land of Transjordan as excellent pasture land for their livestock, propose that this land be set aside for them (Numbers 32:5). Moses rebukes them for the suggestion: "Are your brothers to go to war while you stay here? Why will you turn the minds of the Israelites from crossing into the land that the Lord has given them? That is what your fathers did when I sent them from Kadesh-barnea to survey the land" (Numbers 32:6–8).

Reuben and Gad respond that they will participate in the conquest of the land: "We will build here sheepfolds for our flocks and towns for our children. And we will hasten as shock-troops in the van of the Israelites until we have established them in their home" (Numbers 32:16–17). Moses accepts the proposal, reversing the order of prebattle activity: "Build towns for your children and sheepfolds for your flocks" (Numbers 32:24). The well-being of their dependents must precede the focus on their livestock.

RECAP OF THE WILDERNESS MARCH

Chapter 33 records forty-two stations of the itinerary of the Israelites, starting at Ramses and reaching the Jordan. Shai Held cites a variety of classical explanations for including such a list, ranging from underscoring God's kindness to establishing Israel's merit for following God through the wilderness. He suggests—quite simply, but elegantly—that perhaps the list is designed "to teach a subtle but critical lesson: We can know God, and serve God, at every stop along our way."[15] Godly conduct is not bound by time or place.

APPORTIONMENT OF THE LAND: CITIES OF REFUGE

Although apportionment of the land had been earlier discussed, the election of Reuben and Gad, joined by part of the tribe of Manasseh, to settle in Transjordan required revisiting the apportionment of the land of Canaan. The division of Canaan is taken up in Numbers 33:50–35:8. Following this assignment of land, the Torah discusses cities of refuge.

Jacob Milgrom notes that the institution of blood vengeance was prevalent in the ancient Near East. Commonly, the blood of the slain would be avenged by his nearest kinsman (*go'el*: redeemer). The *go'el* would kill the slayer, or a member of the slayer's family, or he would accept monetary compensation. The Torah's system (Numbers 35:9–34) departed from prevailing practice in the following ways:

1. Only the guilty party is involved; thus, no other member of his family may be slain.
2. Guilt is determined by the slayer's intention: The involuntary homicide is not put to death.
3. The murderer may not pay ransom for his own life to avoid execution.
4. The verdict of deliberate or involuntary homicide is made by the state and not by the bereaved kinsman, and to this end asylum cities for the homicide are established.
5. His trial is by a national tribunal and not by the kinsmen of either party.
6. The deliberate homicide is executed by the *go'el*, and the involuntary homicide is banished to the asylum until the death of the High Priest.[16]

The Torah makes it clear that both murder and accidental killing pollute the land (Numbers 35:33). Shai Held notes that the Torah's insistence on the death of a willful murderer is a reflection of its emphasis on the "incalculable worth of (all) human beings. The point is that one may never place a monetary value on human life." He adds: "Whereas ancient Near Eastern law is lenient in dealing with homicide and strict with crimes against property, biblical law is lenient with offenses against property and severe in confronting cases of homicide."[17]

Though it closes with an eye on "next chapters"—living in the land of Israel—the Book of Numbers is chiefly devoted to the opportunities and challenges of living in community. Community can be a source of strength and blessing; it can also be fraught with polarization and tension. Communities can nurture and strengthen noble ideals; they can devolve into petty bickering and self-destructive behaviors. It is on that backdrop and with the aim of ensuring an enduring future of the people Israel in the land of Israel that Moses, in the book that follows, imparts his closing messages to the generation that stands at the threshold of the Promised Land.

Chapter 8

Jewish Peoplehood

The Book of Numbers relates to years of desert wandering, during which the Israelite tribes lived in community, not always without challenge or internal dispute. The Israelites, as they proceed toward the Promised Land, are individuals, members of tribes and part of a collective "Children of Israel," charged to become a "kingdom of priests and a holy nation." The Torah projects both the importance of each individual and the value of community.

Over time, as a people settled in its land, "the Jews (Judeans) of antiquity constituted an *ethnos*, an ethnic group. They were a named group, attached to a specific territory, whose members shared a sense of common origins, claimed a common and distinctive history and destiny, possessed one or more distinctive characteristics, and felt a sense of collective uniqueness and solidarity."[1] Though the most distinctive among the distinguishing characteristics of the Jews was their religious worship, Jewishness, as Shaye Cohen notes, included far more than religion.

Famously, when, in the Book of Ruth, Ruth, a Moabite woman, insists on attaching herself to her mother-in-law's (Judean) nation, she says, "your people shall be my people, and your God my God" (Ruth 1:16). Religion was part of but not the totality of the Jewish *ethnos*, and Jewishness was lived in community. As we have seen, the *mitzvot* of the Torah extend not only to rituals that might commonly be considered "religious" in the sense in which the word is commonly used but to every aspect of life.

David Hartman aptly notes that "mitzvah is not a private spiritual language but rather a collective language embracing the spiritual needs and capacities of the community."[2] It is on the basis of shared *mitzvot* that individuals build a joint spiritual life. Each individual can, Hartman adds, find new layers of personal meaning in shared concepts and practices.

Diaspora Jewish communities existed throughout the Second Temple period. Migration from Judea escalated, however, following the destruction of the Second Temple and even more so in the aftermath of the Bar Kochba War. Jewish communities were established in an ever-expanding number of settings, and diverse Jewish cultures developed. Yet as David Biale observes in his introduction to *Cultures of the Jews*, despite the diversity of cultures from place to place and period to period, "the Jews throughout the ages believed themselves to have a common national biography and a common culture. . . . On both the popular and elite level . . . the Jewish people were, at once, one and diverse."[3]

While prayer is personal, Jewish tradition directs individuals to assemble in community for worship; in fact, certain prayers are only to be recited in the presence of a *minyan* (a prayer quorum). Heschel observes that "the worth of public worship depends upon the depth of private worship, of the private worship of those who worship together."[4] There is a mutually reinforcing relationship between the individual and the community.

In the Hellenistic and early Roman periods (2,000–2,200 years ago), the term "synagogue" referred to the Jewish community as well as its main building. By the second century CE, the term universally applied to the building in which communal activities were held.[5] Lee Levine, a scholar of the development of the synagogue in antiquity, notes that, over time—during the five-hundred-year period after 70 CE (the destruction of the Temple in Jerusalem)—"the synagogue evolved from a community center with a religious component into a house of worship that included an array of communal activities."[6]

Describing the changing role of the synagogue in Jewish life, Levine writes:

There is no dimension more reflective of the growth and evolution of the synagogue in antiquity than its liturgy. From constituting one of many activities in its early stages, the ritual component of the synagogue eventually became a dominant and definitive element. At first it included the reading of Scriptures, a translation of the reading, and some sort of homily or instruction; by late antiquity, the liturgy had evolved into a rich and varied worship setting which included not only these three components, but also regular communal prayers and poetic recitations (*piyyutim*), especially on Sabbath and holidays.[7]

The synagogue came to provide a common framework and a measure of unity in Jewish life, notwithstanding linguistic, geographical, and cultural variation.[8]

Within the various settings in which Jews lived, whether in the Christian lands of Europe or the Islamic lands of the Near East, considerable authority over internal Jewish affairs was vested in Jewish communal leadership structures. Typically, the ruling power recognized this internal, regulatory authority. The Jewish community paid taxes raised in accordance with rules established and enforced by its autonomous governance mechanisms.

In addition to collecting Jewish communal taxes remitted to the ruling authority, Jewish communities maintained a variety of funds for support of indigent Jews. For example, Maimonides codifies (*Mishneh Torah*, Seeds, Laws of Gifts to the Poor 9:1) that "every Jewish community must appoint collectors of *tzedakah* (charity) who are trustworthy men of repute, to go about the people each Friday, taking from every one what he can afford to give, or what he is assessed. They are to distribute the money Friday to Friday, giving every poor man sufficient food for seven days. This is what is called *kuppah*." Beyond the fund for food, additional assessments were levied for such needs as clothing and burial (*Mishneh Torah*, Seeds, Laws of Gifts to the Poor 9:12).

Discipline was maintained through *ḥerem*, the power of Jewish authorities to ban or excommunicate a noncompliant community member; the threat of *ḥerem*, by and large, ensured enforcement of communal norms. In contrast, a hallmark of modernity was individual citizenship, and the concomitant erosion and abolition of Jewish communal authority structures (just as corporate units, generally, were dismantled). Jewish affiliation and, for that matter, identity, has become, over time, entirely voluntary.

Just as, in nineteenth-century Western Europe, Reform, Positive Historical (Conservative), and Orthodox Judaism emerged in response to currents of enlightenment and emancipation; in Eastern Europe, Hasidism, a movement that popularized Jewish mysticism and emphasized ecstatic religiosity and communion with God, emerged as a response to changing social, economic, and political conditions. Israel ben Eliezer (1700–1760), known as the Baal Shem Tov (master of the good name), and the Hasidic teachers who followed emphasized individual, spiritual redemption. Yet the individual Hasid's spiritual quest takes place within community. The relationship between the individual and the community is an enduring part of Jewish thought and experience, magnified in an era of voluntary association.

Mordecai Kaplan's magnum opus, *Judaism as a Civilization: Toward a Reconstruction of American-Jewish Life*, was not only descriptive of the reality that Jewishness is not exclusively a matter of religious belief and practice, it offered an agenda for constructing new, voluntary communal forms in an open society.[9] Notwithstanding Kaplan's impact, expressed in part through a proliferation of "Synagogue Centers" and Jewish Community Centers during the second and third quarters of the twentieth century, American society—Jews included—is increasingly individualistic. In their work *The Jew Within*, Steven M. Cohen and Arnold Eisen, whose conclusions were drawn from extensive personal interviews, note that "the first language that our subjects speak is by and large one of profound individualism."[10]

Reflecting on contemporary challenges to building commitment to Jewish community, Jonathan Woocher perceptively points to two related phenomena:

> On the one hand, we see an accentuation of individualism, personalism, and choice as dominant features in our society and culture. This thrust, epitomized in what has been called the "sovereign self," undermines all *a priori* loyalties and especially loyalty to collectives that are perceived as seeking to impose limits on personal freedom or as setting standards for behavior that contravene the ultimate decision-making power of the individual. On the other hand, we also witness today, especially among young people, a heightened commitment to globalism, multi-culturalism, and universalism. This commitment renders what might be seen as particularistic loyalties—e.g., loyalty to a specific ethnic group or nation—as morally problematic. Why should we single out members of one community or one people for special concern when so many need so much?[11]

Woocher reminds us, though, that people inherently seek connection with others and to something beyond themselves, and that the Jewish story is of a people dedicated to righteousness and justice with a vision and goal of universal redemption.

Jonathan Krasner suggests the need "to find a new equilibrium between the individual search for meaning and the imperative of living for something larger than oneself."[12] Finding personal meaning within community is an enduring dimension of Jewishness. It offers rich dividends of personal fulfillment as well as contributing to the advancement of the universal goal that is the ultimate mission of the Jewish people.

Though Jewishness has always been pluralistic and multivocal, in the contemporary era Jewish identity has become far more fluid than at any time since antiquity. Shaye Cohen notes that "the uncertainty of Jewishness in antiquity curiously prefigures the uncertainty of Jewishness in modern times."[13] However, he adds, there is a major difference:

> The major difference between our world and theirs is that the existential contrast between Us and Them was a reality for the Jews of antiquity, even for the pre-rabbinic Jews and the non-rabbinic Jews, whereas it is not a reality for many contemporary Jews of the diaspora. The majority of the Jews of the United States, perhaps the vast majority, do not feel alienated from gentile society. Certainly our neutral society does nothing to reinforce Jewish identity or to compel Jews to remain Jews.[14]

Cohen described prevailing social conditions at the close of the twentieth century. By the 2020s, there was, unfortunately, an uptick in anti-Semitic rhetoric in the United States, and reported incidents of anti-Semitism were on the rise. The possible impact of this unfortunate current on the Jewish consciousness of American Jews remains to be assessed.

Milton Steinberg identifies the three "ingredients" of Jewishness as religion, culture, and peoplehood. For Steinberg, peoplehood "is the motif that persists when the others have been dissipated. By virtue of this a Jew may renounce the Jewish faith and repudiate Jewish culture, and remain both subjectively and objectively a Jew by identity. He is still part of the Jewish people."[15]

Donniel Hartman notes that "Judaism is primarily a modality of being and belonging, an ethnic identity with a strong collective consciousness."[16] This collective consciousness often translates to a sense of kinship and mutual responsibility referred to as *areivut*. Jewish peoplehood, a theme of the Book of Numbers, is, for many Jews, a most meaningful dimension of Jewishness.

Particularly at times of crisis, a heightened sense of *areivut*, responsibility for the welfare and well-being of other Jews, is evident. One example in recent decades is the efforts of American Jews and Jews around the globe on behalf of Soviet Jewry that contributed to the exodus of 1.5 million Jews from Russia, 1989 to 2006. More recently, substantial numbers of Jews responded in various ways to the murder, on a single day, of twelve hundred people and the kidnapping of hundreds of others by Hamas terrorists in October 2023. Whether through financial support, political activism, religious expression, or a combination of such responses, peoplehood and a sense of responsibility for one's kin evokes community consciousness and action. Synagogues, Jewish Federations, and myriad Jewish organizations—each a voluntary coming together of individual Jews joined in common purpose—reflect continuing group consciousness among many American Jews, well into the twenty-first century.

Jewish liturgy powerfully expresses concern for the welfare of Jews who might be in peril at any time, in any locale. In a prayer traditionally recited Monday and Thursday mornings during public worship, before returning the Torah to the ark, the congregation recites: "As for our brothers of the whole house of Israel who are in distress or captivity, on sea or land, may the All-Present have compassion on them and lead them from distress to relief, from darkness to light, and from oppression to freedom, now, swiftly, and soon."

The term *k'lal yisrael* refers to the totality of the Jewish people, the collective whole. There are diverse communities of Jews even in the same locales, and there are Jewish individuals who live apart from community; all are part of *k'lal yisrael*. Both the dignity of the individual and responsibility to the community are embedded in the Torah; their interplay is, as the Torah itself, dynamic. The search for a "new equilibrium" between the individual Jew and the Jewish collective, the relationship between Jews who live in Israel and Jews who live in other lands, relationships between Jews of differing outlooks, and the relationship of Jewish communities to the societies of which they are a part, are all vital components of the Jewish conversation in the twenty-first century.

Chapter 9

The Book of Deuteronomy

Jewish Learning, from Generation to Generation

Deuteronomy, known in Hebrew as *D'varim* (words), is also called *Mishneh Torah* (repetition of the Torah). It is the latter name, drawn from Deuteronomy 17:18, that yields the Greek word *Deuteronomion* (second law) that is Deuteronomy in English. The book consists of a series of speeches that Moses addresses to the people Israel in Moab, during the period just prior to his death. He reminds the Israelites that the promise of the land they will shortly enter is conditional; their well-being depends on living in accordance with the laws they have received. It is essential that they study these laws and teach them to their children. Bible scholar Jeffrey Tigay observes that, in expounding the laws of the Torah, Moses, especially in Deuteronomy, often explains the laws' "logic, justice, or consequences."[1]

Though titled a repetition of the law, Deuteronomy incudes many laws not earlier referenced in the Torah. These laws relate to matters associated with living in Israel; they were not, to this point, relevant to the Israelites' experience. Moses delivers a series of discourses, beginning with a review of the Israelites' wandering, proceeds to a presentation of laws, and closes with a farewell address.

MOSES'S FIRST DISCOURSE (DEUT. 1–4:43)

Moses's first discourse begins with an historical retrospective and then focuses on the importance of living by the teachings of the Torah. He reminds the people of how it came to pass that he installed judges: "chiefs of thousands, chiefs of hundreds, chiefs of fifties, and chiefs of tens, and officials for your tribes" (Deut. 1:15). Moses charges the judges with carrying out the following instructions: "Hear out your fellow men, and decide justly between any man and a fellow Israelite or stranger. You shall not be partial in judgment: hear out the low and high alike. Fear no man, for judgment is God's" (Deut. 1:16–17).

Focusing on the latter part of Moses's directive, Shai Held comments that Moses conveys to his generation and subsequent readers of the Torah text that "the kind of society (or community) they (and us) will have depends on the kind of leaders they have. Wisdom and acuity are critical, as are uprightness and a commitment to justice, including (and perhaps especially) justice for the weak and vulnerable. And yet, Moses warns, all of this will come to naught without one vital, indispensable virtue: the courage to say and do what is right regardless of who will disagree or disapprove."[2]

Reflecting on an underlying message of Moses's discourses, Jeffrey Tigay observes:

> Every parent is to be a teacher of religion. This obligation is the most pervasive expression of the biblical conviction that religion is not simply a personal, individual concern. Deuteronomy emphasizes repeatedly that the Israelites are not to keep to themselves the experience they had and the responsibilities they were taught: they must transmit them to their children and grandchildren so that they, too, may share in the experiences, learn their responsibilities, and enjoy the benefits of faith and observance.[3]

Nehama Leibowitz calls attention to instructions given to refrain from contending with the children of Esau (Deut. 2:4–6) as well as the Moabites and Ammonites. She observes that "a reverse test faced the children of those who had died in the wilderness, that of the strong versus the weak, that of resisting the temptation to take advantage of their superior strength by harassing their weaker neighbors."[4] Moses declares: "See, I have imparted to you laws and rules . . . for you to abide by in the land" (Deut. 4:5). On its face, the statement relates to observance of certain laws—particularly, those based on agriculture—that have specific application to the land of Israel. The Hebrew, *be-kerev ha-aretz*, has the connotation "in the midst of the land." Homiletically, the verse can be understood to express the message that the road to holiness is within society, not by living as a recluse, separated from community.

Moses reminds the Israelites that they are a nation distinguished by its God and by its law. Observing the teachings of Torah, he says, "will be proof of your wisdom and discernment to other peoples, who on hearing of all these laws will say, 'Surely, that great nation is a wise and discerning people'" (Deut. 4:6). It is essential, Moses emphasizes, that the Israelites not forget God's teachings or their people's experiences, and that they "make them known to your children and to your children's children" (Deut. 4:9).

MOSES'S SECOND DISCOURSE (DEUT. 4:44–28:69)

Continuing the theme of the importance of Torah study, Moses declares: "Hear, O Israel, the laws and rules that I proclaim to you this day! Study them and observe them faithfully!" (Deut. 5:1). He reminds the Israelites of an enduring covenant and repeats—with slight differences in wording from the text that appears in Exodus 20—the Decalogue (Deut. 5:6–18). He then shifts his focus from the experience at Mount Sinai to the present, in Moab.

Moses enjoins the Israelites to obey God's laws and commandments. He reminds them of God's unity and uniqueness, pronouncing: "Hear, O Israel! The Lord is God, the Lord alone" (Deut. 6:4). This declaration, *Sh'ma* (hear), is followed immediately by the exhortation *Ve-ahavta*, "You shall love the Lord your God" (Deut. 6:5). Love of God is not simply a matter of emotional attachment, it is to be expressed in right conduct.

After repeatedly admonishing the Israelites to obey God's commandments, Moses calls upon them to "do what is right and good in the sight of the Lord" (Deut. 6:18). Rashi explains "right and good" as requiring compromise to resolve disputes, acting beyond the letter of the law. Ramban notes that the Torah could not possibly have detailed every conceivable human interaction. The declaration that God loves the good and the upright is a call to always act in accordance with principles of holiness and righteousness. Nehama Leibowitz, quoting twentieth-century Rabbi Yeshaya Shapiro, writes that "whoever wishes to achieve a perfect observance of the Torah cannot rest content with adhering to its explicit rulings. He must penetrate deeper to arrive at the ultimate aim of these rulings. He must not only think of what is good and upright in his own eyes but that which is 'upright and good in the eyes of the Lord.'"[5]

Carrying forward the theme of education, Moses observes that successive generations will surely ask about the Torah's instructions and Israel's way of life. In a passage that features prominently in the Passover *haggadah*, parents are summoned to recall the experience of slavery in Egypt and redemption from bondage. Israel's covenant, of which the Torah is a foundational expression, is associated with this collective narrative.

Moses instructs that, when the Israelites enter the beautiful land and eat their fill, "give thanks to the Lord your God for the good land which He has given you" (Deut. 8:10). This verse serves as the basis for the practice of reciting *birkat ha-mazon*, the blessing after meals. Moses calls attention to the potential peril of prosperity (Deut. 8:11–20). "Beware lest your heart grow haughty and you forget the Lord your God—who freed you from the land of Egypt, the house of bondage" (Deut. 8:14). The Israelites must not "say to yourselves, 'My own power and the might of my own hand have won this wealth for me.' Remember that it is the Lord your God who gives you the power to get wealth, in fulfillment of the covenant that He made an oath with your fathers, as is still the case" (Deut. 8:17–18).

Moses presents a guiding principle through a question and response: "And now, O Israel, what does the Lord your God demand of you? Only this: to revere the Lord your God, to walk only in His paths, to love Him, and to serve the Lord your God with all your heart and soul, keeping the Lord's commandments and laws, which I enjoin upon you today, for your good" (Deut. 10:12–13). Love of God is expressed through Godly action. As God "upholds the cause of the fatherless and the widow, and befriends the stranger, providing him with food and clothing. You too must befriend the stranger, for you were strangers in the land of Egypt" (Deut. 10:18–19).

Moses reminds the Israelites that remembering God's teachings and instructing their children accordingly is essential to their continuing prosperity in the land. Unlike irrigation in Egypt, the land of Israel depends on rain; if God withholds rain in response to the community's disobedience, Israel will perish from the land (Deut. 11:10–17). In contrast to Moses's earlier exhortation to "love the Lord your God" (Deut. 6:5–9), Deuteronomy 11:13–20, which constitutes the second passage recited after *Sh'ma yisrael* in traditional Jewish liturgy, is written in the plural. A wicked society, Moses observes, will not long endure.

Deuteronomy 11:26 begins with a singular verb addressed to the entire people Israel, a plural subject: "You see" (singular), "I set before you" (plural) blessing and curse. The opportunity of heeding the teachings presented by Moses is, ultimately, a matter of individual choice. Though Moses instructs all Israel, each person must, in the final analysis, elect to take advantage (or not) of the benefit set before the entire community.

In chapter 12 of Deuteronomy, Moses instructs the Israelites not to worship in like manner as the Canaanites. Rather, "look only to the site that the Lord your God will choose amidst all your tribes as His habitation, to establish His name there. There you are to go, and there you are to bring your burnt offerings and other sacrifices, your tithes and contributions, your votive and freewill offerings, and the firstlings of your herds and flocks. Together with your households, you shall feast there before the Lord your God, happy in all the undertakings in which the Lord your God has blessed you" (Deut. 12:5–7). Jeffrey Tigay notes that "Deuteronomy stresses the effect that the offerings have on people rather than any effect they might have on God."[6]

Following an exhortation about false prophets and those who might entice the people to stray from the legacy of Torah, Moses directs: "Follow none but the Lord your God, and revere none but Him . . . and hold fast to Him" (Deut. 13:5). In the face of currents that might entirely undermine the foundations of Torah teaching, Moses encourages collective moral resistance.

The Torah instructs the people Israel not to cut or gash themselves: "*lo titgodedu*" (Deut. 14:1). While this directive, in context, is a ban on the pagan practice of physical cutting, rabbinic teaching suggests another dimension of understanding this *mitzvah*. Contentiousness and bickering should not cut up the people Israel, destroying its sense of unity.

Chapter 14 proceeds to a section on dietary regulations, listing permitted and prohibited animals, fish, and fowl (14:3–21). The text then turns to tithe obligations, release of debts, and *tzedakah* (laws of charity). Four years out of seven the tithe is to be consumed by the farmer and his household at the sanctuary that God will choose. In the third and sixth year of each seven-year cycle, the tithe is dedicated to feeding the Levites (who are landless) and the poor; on the seventh year of each cycle, the land lies fallow.

Chapter 15 includes a remarkable sequence of verses relating to economic life—the ideal and the real—in the land of Israel. Deuteronomy 15:4 reads: "There shall be no needy among you—since the Lord your God will bless you in the land that the Lord your God is giving you as a hereditary portion." Yet, just a few lines later, the Torah instructs: "If, however, there is a needy person among you . . . you must open your hand and lend him sufficient for whatever he needs" (Deut. 15:7–8). Though, in an ideal world, there would be no poverty, "there will never cease to be needy ones in your land" (Deut. 15:11), and provisions must be made to ensure that people are assisted.

The word *tzedakah*, commonly translated as "charity," comes from the Hebrew word for justice, *tzedek*. While the Latin root of charity and the Greek words rendered as philanthropy refer to love of man, *tzedakah* is anchored in the notion of justice. Whether or not one feels love or compassion for another—that is, whether or not one is "moved" to be charitable to another—the Torah prescribes *tzedakah* as a duty.

Deuteronomy 16:1–17 describes the three pilgrimage festivals earlier referenced in the Torah. Common themes are commemoration of the exodus and the expression of gratitude for the harvest. The repetition in the Book of Deuteronomy includes the instruction that these festivals are to be observed at the designated sanctuary.

Turning to the appointment of judges and officials, Moses directs: "Justice, justice shall you pursue" (Deut. 16:20). Not only is justice to be vigorously pursued, just ends are to be pursued through just means. Beyond merely pronouncing justice as a value, the Torah applies the concept in concrete terms through specific laws. The pursuit of justice is an essential condition for Israel's thriving in the Promised Land.

When disputes arise, litigants are to "appear before the levitical priests, or the magistrate in charge at the time" (Deut. 17:9). Judges must not only be well-versed in the law, they must be familiar with each generation's particular circumstances; hence, "at the time." The religious authorities of each generation have applied the Torah to the situations arising in their time, recognizing this as a sacred responsibility.

The Torah anticipates that, after settling in the land of Israel, the Israelites will decide to establish a monarchy. The Torah prescribes that the king is to write "a copy of this Teaching. . . . Let it remain with him and let him read in it all his life" (Deut. 17:18–19). The king is not above the law; he is constantly to remind himself that he is subject to the teachings of the Torah. "The aim of the law," writes Jeffrey Tigay, "is to limit the king's power and to characterize him as essentially an optional figurehead who is as much subject to God's law as are the people as a whole."[7]

Shai Held calls attention to the closing verse of this passage: "to the end that he (the king) and his descendants may reign long in the midst of Israel" (Deut. 17:20). Not only does the king remain one of the people, "always 'in their midst' . . . dynastic rule is entirely conditional. The king and his descendants will maintain the throne only as long as they are faithful to the covenant."[8]

The last of the laws dealing with public officials is a complex ceremony for removing blood guilt when an unidentified murder victim is found in the outskirts of a community. The ritual of slaughtering a heifer and declaring "our hands did not shed this blood, nor did our eyes see it done" (Deut. 21:7) is puzzling. The Talmud comments: "Would we ever have imagined that the Beth Din [referring to the elders] were shedders of blood? But what they implied was: No one came within our jurisdiction whom we discharged without food and whom we left without providing him an escort" (Sotah 46b). Nehama Leibowitz adds:

We may note here that the concept of "bloodshed" is interpreted here in a very broad manner to include even indirect responsibility for the death of a human being through neglect to attend to his elementary needs. The public as a whole and the city nearest to the slain and its elders are all responsible for the terrible deed committed in the field. Their whole way of life, their social order, economic, educational and security institutions are answerable for the murder. The guilt is not confined merely to the individual perpetrator. The whole of society is directly involved.[9]

Deuteronomy 21:10–14 addresses marriage with a woman captured in war. Commenting on this Torah-sanctioned practice, theologian Shai

Held observes: "It would be a grave error to assume that marrying a captive is something the Torah wants soldiers to do; it is rather something it permits them to do because it assumes that, bad as it is, it is a better outcome than soldiers simply raping captive women and then abandoning them."[10] Quoting the Talmud's statement that "the Torah was not given to the ministering angels" (Me'ilah 14b), Held suggests that "some biblical laws are attempts to make the best of a very bad situation, to introduce (and demand) a modicum of humanity into what are objectively ugly and degraded circumstances." He opines that "in the struggle to affirm the value, dignity, and rights of women, we engage in a process set in motion and thus sanctioned by the Torah itself."[11]

Deuteronomy 21:18–21 discusses punishment—by stoning—of a wayward and defiant son. The Talmud, based on close reading of the biblical verses relating to the matter, attaches so many requirements to arrive at such an outcome that the sages conclude that there never was nor will there ever be a capital case of this sort (Sanhedrin 71a). Chapter 22 opens with the *mitzvah* of returning lost property. The Jerusalem Talmud (Bava Metzia 2:5) tells of a Roman emperor whose wife lost a piece of jewelry. A reward was announced for return of the object within thirty days; anyone found in possession of it after thirty days was subject to decapitation. Rabbi Shmuel, who happened to find the object early on, waited until after the thirty-day period to return it. When queried by the empress as to why he had waited to return the article, he replied: "One should not say that I acted out of fear of you, but out of fear of the Merciful." The empress, the Talmud relates, exclaimed: "Praised is the God of the Jews."

Chapter 22:6–7 presents the *mitzvah* of chasing away the mother bird rather than taking the mother bird with her young. This passage bespeaks the value of avoiding *tza'ar ba'alei hayim*, causing unnecessary pain to animals. Similarly, the Torah prescribes that "you shall not plow with an ox and an ass together" (Deut. 22:10), presumably because they differ greatly in size and strength. Later (Deut. 25:4), the Torah prohibits muzzling an ox while it is threshing, an act of cruelty to animals. So abhorrent is dishonesty that the Torah forbids owning, let alone using, inaccurate weights and measures (Deut. 25:14). Rather, "You must have completely honest weights and completely honest measures, if you are to endure long on the soil that the Lord your God is giving you" (Deut. 25:15).

Chapter 26 begins by describing a ceremony for bringing first fruits "to the place where the Lord your God will choose to establish His name" (Deut. 26:2). A liturgical pronouncement of gratitude is to be recited, acknowledging God as the source of bounty: "My father was a fugitive Aramean. He went down to Egypt with meager numbers and sojourned there; but there he became a great and very populous nation. The Egyptians dealt harshly with us and oppressed us; they imposed heavy labor upon us. We cried to the Lord, the God of our fathers, and the Lord heard our plea and saw our plight, our misery, and our oppression. The Lord freed us from Egypt by a mighty hand, by an outstretched arm and awesome power, and by signs and portents. He brought us to this place and gave us this land, a land flowing with milk and honey. Wherefore I now bring the first fruits of the soil which You, O Lord, have given me" (Deut. 26:5–10).

The pilgrim who brings first fruits is to enjoy the bounty God has given him "together with the Levite and the stranger in your midst" (Deut. 26:11) and to share a tenth of his yield with "the Levite, the stranger, the fatherless, and the widow" (Deut. 26:12). As Shai Held aptly notes, "The Torah here makes a radical point, central to its social and theological vision: Genuine gratitude to God always leads to generosity and the desire to share our blessing with others."[12] *Hakarat ha-tov*—acknowledgment of the good that we daily enjoy—is nurtured through the expression of thanks for the gifts that we all too often take for granted.

Moses proclaims: "The Lord your God commands you this day to observe these laws and rules" (Deut. 26:16). Such instructions, though, were ostensibly communicated nearly forty years earlier. The generation about to cross the Jordan River had never experienced living in Israel nor had the opportunity of performing *mitzvot*—such as those associated with first fruits—uniquely connected to that setting. The covenant is therefore reaffirmed: "You have affirmed this day that the Lord is your God, that you will walk in His ways, that you will observe His laws and commandments and rules, and that you will obey Him. And the Lord has affirmed this day that you are, as He promised you, His treasured people who shall observe all His commandments" (Deut. 26:17–18).

Deuteronomy 27:2–3 instructs that, on the day the Israelites cross the Jordan, "you shall set up large stones . . . and inscribe upon them all the words of this Teaching." Interestingly, these stones are to be erected on Mount Ebal (Deut. 27:4). Just a few verses later (Deut. 27:12–13), a passage of blessings and curses is presented, the blessings pronounced from Mount Gerizim and the curses from Mount Ebal. Moreover, Mount Gerizim was fertile and Mount Ebal barren. Why place stones with teachings of Torah on Mount Ebal? Samson Raphael Hirsch suggests that the possibility of spiritual growth is not dependent on material conditions. Even the poor soil of Mount Ebal could serve as a platform for Torah.

In identifying the consequences associated with failure to live in accordance with the teachings of Torah, the text (Deut. 28:47–48) reads: "Because you would not serve the Lord your God in joy and gladness over the abundance of everything, you shall have to serve—in hunger and thirst, naked and lacking everything—the enemies whom the Lord will let loose against you." Happiness, the Torah teaches, is an essential part of the service of God.

MOSES'S THIRD DISCOURSE (DEUT. 29:1–30:20)

Moses conveys that the covenant binds all generations. "I make this covenant with its sanctions, not with you alone, but with those who are standing here with us this day before the Lord our God and with those who are not with us here this day" (Deut. 29:13–14). Though, at times, the people Israel might be banished from the land of its ancestors, the land of Israel is an integral part of the covenant. "God will restore your fortunes and take you back in love. . . . And the Lord your God will bring you to the land that your fathers possessed, and you shall possess it" (Deut. 30:3–5).

The teachings of Torah are accessible to all; they are not out of reach. In Moses's words: "Surely, this Instruction which I enjoin upon you this day is not too baffling for you, nor is it beyond reach. It is not in the heavens, that you should say, 'Who among us can go up to the heavens and get it for us and impart it to us, that we may observe it? Neither is it beyond the sea" (Deut. 30:11–13).

Moses adjures the people Israel to walk in God's ways. "I have put before you life and death, blessing and curse. Choose life—if you and your offspring would live—by loving the Lord your God, heeding His commands and holding fast to Him. For thereby you shall have life and shall long endure on the soil that the Lord swore to your ancestors, Abraham, Isaac, and Jacob, to give to them" (Deut. 30:19–20).

MOSES'S LAST DAYS

Moses calls Joshua and charges him to "be strong and resolute, for it is you who shall go with this people into the land that the Lord swore to their fathers to give them, and it is you who shall apportion it to them" (Deut. 31:7). Moses writes down "this Teaching" and instructs that, every seventh year, at the holiday of Sukkot, "you shall read this Teaching aloud in the presence of all Israel" (Deut. 31:10–11). Not only adults, but "their children, too . . . shall hear and learn to revere the Lord your God" (Deut. 31:13). While the children—particularly, the very young—might not understand the particulars of what is expressed, the experience of the gathering will leave an impression and serve as an inspiring memory.

This gathering, known as *hak'hel*, takes place at the beginning of the *shemittah* year when the land lies fallow and debts are remitted. Shai Held comments that, though Israel's covenant is about serving God, it is also about creating a loving and just community.

> Once every seven years, the Torah beckons us back to Sinai. In the process it reminds us of—it actively enacts for us—the essence of communal living. Despite the illusions fostered by social and economic inequality, we are all brothers and sisters in the covenant. And despite the fantasy that we are untouchable, safe behind an impregnable fortress—as if we have somehow transcended the irreducible fragility of human life—we are all vulnerable and dependent. That realization makes it possible to acknowledge both the depth of our debt to God and the profundity of our connection to each other.[13]

In chapter 32, Moses addresses the people Israel in poetry, calling upon heaven and earth, enduring witnesses, as he reprises the theme of God's greatness and the unreliability of the Israelites. He urges the people Israel to recall and learn from their past. "Remember the days of old, Consider the years of ages past; Ask your father, he will inform you, Your elders, they will tell you" (Deut. 32:7).

Moses hears God's voice summoning him to ascend Mount Nebo: "You may view the land from a distance, but you shall not enter it—the land that I am giving to the Israelite people" (Deut. 32:52). Chapter 33 is "the blessing with which Moses, the man of God, bade the Israelites farewell before he died" (Deut. 33:1). This is followed by Moses's ascending Mount Nebo, viewing "the land of which I swore to Abraham, Isaac, and Jacob" (Deut. 34:4). There Moses dies, and "no one knows his burial place to this day" (Deut. 34:6). Shai Held insightfully expresses an enduring lesson from the Torah's account of Moses's life and passing. "In his death, as in his life, Moses is the model of covenantal living—a tireless servant of God and Israel who dies before reaching the place of which he dreams each day. Moses's life teaches us that to live covenantally is to live in the present, toward the future."[14]

In this closing book of the Torah, the importance of learning and teaching the ideals of Torah throughout the generations is underscored. In the words of Jonathan Sacks: "Moses realized that a people achieves immortality not by building temples or mausoleums, but by engraving their values on the hearts of their children, and they on theirs, and so on until the end of time."[15] Those values include an abiding connection with the land of Israel, a sense of covenantal imperatives, a commitment to pursuit of *kedushah* (sanctification), identification with and responsibility as part of the Jewish collective (*klal yisrael*), and lifelong engagement in Jewish learning. It is these overarching values that are central to the five books that comprise the Torah.

Chapter 10

Jewish Education

A Lifelong Journey

Moses exhorts the people Israel to instruct successive generations. For millennia, in widely scattered places, and under varying conditions, Jews instructed their children concerning the teachings and practices of Jewish life, enabling them to negotiate their way as Jews. Educational opportunities were typically gender based, and there was by no means equal education for all. That said, Jews had a penchant for learning that was recognized by those outside their circle. A twelfth-century monk observed: "The Jews, out of their zeal for God and their love of the Law, put as many sons as they have to letters, that each may understand God's law. . . . A Jew, however poor, if he had ten sons, would put them all to letters, not for gain, as the Christians do, but for the understanding of God's Law, and not only his sons but his daughters."[1]

Though perhaps exaggerated to support the cleric's call for greater attention to learning among the Christian faithful, the sense of the observation was reflected in communal mechanisms in many times and places to ensure access to some measure of Jewish education. Family life and communal norms served to provide and reinforce Jewish learning. In the most recent generations, Jewish education, as Jewish practice and Jewish identification, is voluntary.

It is the premise of this book that those of Jewish heritage do well to access and learn from Jewish wisdom reflected in its texts, starting with the Torah. Jewish education can, through the rich resources of Jewish teaching, help learners "achieve a more meaningful, connected, and fulfilling life," enabling them to "answer their authentic questions and experience the mix of joy, purposefulness, wonder, invigoration, and peacefulness that most humans seek."[2] Daniel Gordis comments that "when the Torah tells the story of our ancestors, we discover that the questions that perplex us, the ones that shape our spiritual odysseys, are not new. We discover in grappling with Jewish texts that our fundamental questions are perennial; we learn that the human condition is not a modern condition but a timeless, existential one."[3]

Articulating the aims and desired outcomes of Jewish education, Bible scholar Moshe Greenberg writes: "A Jewish education worthy of the name will address the hunger of the learner to know 'whence he came and whither he is going.' It will furnish him with value-concepts by which to infuse raw experience with meaning and order. The success of a Jewish education is measured by its adequacy in accompanying the learner through life as a treasury of concepts lending meaning to private and public experience."[4]

Much of Jewish education is, today, learner centered, drawing on Jewish wisdom to help students flourish in the world of which they are part. Part of that flourishing is connection to others and to something larger than themselves. The study of Torah enables learners to take part in the ongoing Jewish conversation, to shape the continuing narrative of a covenantal community, and to contribute to the realization of an enduring vision.

A late twentieth-century statement of principles published by the Conservative movement well expresses the value that has traditionally attached to Torah study and its continuing importance:

> *Talmud Torah* (study of Torah, including all classical Jewish texts) is an essential value of Judaism. Virtually alone among all religious traditions, Judaism regards study as a cardinal commandment, the highest form of the worship of God. *Talmud Torah* is the obligation and the privilege of every Jew, male and female, young and old, no matter how much or how little one knows at present. Since following the precepts of Judaism requires that one know its beliefs and practices, and since it is impossible to exhaust the Torah's meaning, each individual Jew is commanded to be a *ben* or *bat* Torah, studying Torah throughout his or her life. According to Talmudic legend, God Himself spends part of His day studying Torah.[5]

Jewish education, the authors of the statement remind us, is not merely a childhood pursuit, but a lifelong journey. Jewish education is by no means exclusively about the study of texts. Jewish learning includes lived experiences, music, arts, and more. As Daniel Gordis notes: "Jewish life has to be experienced. Its power, its majesty, its sensitivity, and its wisdom come alive to Jews when they live it, not when they simply think about it."[6]

Jewish education is of the heart and of the mind. Because of the immersive opportunities they afford, Jewish educational camp experiences—not only for children but for families and adults—can provide powerful learning opportunities. Similarly, one can learn far more about Israel by experiencing it than by (merely) reading a book about it. As in antiquity, synagogues remain places of communal activity and Jewish experience. Three Hebrew terms describe the multiple aspects of contemporary Jewish congregations: *beit tefillah* (house of prayer), *beit midrash* (house of study), and *beit knesset* (house of gathering).

One aspect of Jewish learning—or access to it—that is particularly challenging is mastery of the Hebrew language. Many years ago, I was in Rome for the first time and went to see the Arch of Titus, an arch constructed in honor of the victorious general who destroyed the Second Temple. As I stood at the arch, a Roman Jew began to speak with me in Hebrew (our lone shared language). He told me that, from the time the arch was constructed, the Jews of Rome had never walked through it. Judeans had been brought to Rome in chains and sold as slaves; the Temple and much of Jewish life in Judea was in ruins. For the Jews of Rome, the arch was a symbol of destruction and degradation. On Friday, May 14, 1948, he told me he (as a child) and many other Jews of Rome gathered at the arch and, singing *Hatikvah* ("the hope," a poem that became Israel's national anthem), walked through the arch, after Israel's Declaration of Independence was broadcast. Almost no less remarkable to me than the story of pride in the reestablishment of a sovereign Jewish state was the fact that an Italian Jew and an American Jew were standing at the arch conversing in Hebrew.

Some years later, at a time of reawakening of Jewish consciousness among many Jews in what was then the Soviet Union, my wife and I spent a few weeks in the USSR, surrounding Passover. On May 1 (a national holiday) I gave a lecture to a living room full of Jews, in Kishinev. The talk I gave was, again, in a language we shared: Hebrew. Hebrew was an illegal language in the Soviet Union (my wife's Hebrew/Russian *haggadot* were, for that reason, seized at the airport as contraband on our arrival to the country). Not only did lecture attendees listen to a talk in Hebrew, they asked questions in Hebrew that was more elegant than the speaker's. Apart from admiration of their remarkable act of defiance in having mastered an illegal language, I was again struck by the bond that linked us not only by way of the Jewish history of which I spoke but in the language that our people have shared for millennia (though, to be sure, modern Hebrew, as the State of Israel, is an "Old-New" phenomenon).

The Statement of Principles for Reform Judaism (1999) declares: "We affirm the importance of studying Hebrew, the language of Torah and Jewish liturgy, that we may draw closer to our people's sacred texts."[7] The Conservative movement emphasizes Hebrew in order "to maintain close connection to fellow Jews in Israel and around the world and to have immediate access to sacred texts, the *siddur*, and the record of previous Jewish study and living of Torah."[8] These are aspirational goals with well-considered rationales. The reality is that most American-born individuals—with the exception of those whose parents are immigrants—are monolingual. This extends to Jewish Americans, most of whom do not possess anything beyond familiarity with a limited number of Hebrew words.

Longtime Hebrew Union College professor Michael Meyer comments that "even in the absence of fully developed linguistic capacity, individual Hebrew words can express ideas and values that define the community and which cannot always be rendered adequately by equivalents in other languages. The most minimal Jewish education should at least teach the meaning of key words, mostly in Hebrew but partly also in other Jewish languages, that constitute a vocabulary of Jewish discourse. Obvious examples are Torah, *tefillah* (prayer), and *menschlichkeit* (humaneness; decency)."[9] Such words as *mitzvah, tzedakah, ḥesed, aliyah, halakhah, tikkun olam, k'lal yisrael,* and *areivut* have appeared in this book. Meyers would urge Jews to develop a vocabulary of Hebrew words that reflect key value concepts in Jewish life.

EMBARKING ON THE JOURNEY:
ENRICHING THE CONVERSATION

Many years ago, as a student in middle school, I received the follow-ing "prompt" for an essay: As technology advances, less and less time will be required of people in the workplace. How will people use their expanded leisure time? Fast forward quite a few decades, and not only are people busier than ever, but the changes wrought by technology have not been entirely positive or benign. For example, Jonathan Sacks, notes, "the internet makes it hard for us to distinguish between truth and rumor and is the most effective disseminator of paranoia and hatred yet invented."[10] Similarly, artificial intelligence can be deployed for posi-tive purposes but can also be manipulated to spread misinformation.

At a time of heightened scientific and technological advances, the search for meaning is no less compelling than in ages past. "To find meaning in life is to find something we are called on to do," writes Sacks. "Science is the search for explanation. Religion is the search for meaning," he continues.[11] Judaism is a call to action; in Heschel's words: "Judaism stands and falls with the idea of the absolute relevance of human deeds."[12]

The Torah begins with the world that God—portrayed in the Torah as a commanding Power with will and consciousness, manifesting moral goodness, and in relationship with humankind—created. It proceeds to what humankind, endowed with freedom, can make of the world. The Torah points to a connection with Israel, a call to covenantal relation-ship (emphasizing responsibility rather than, exclusively, rights) and purposeful action in history, sanctification of all aspects of life, with associated performative acts (meaning-filled rituals), the importance of community, and ongoing engagement in Jewish learning as strands in the tapestry of Jewish living.

It is certainly possible to live as a Jew without embracing all of these strands. There are Jews, for example, who deeply engage with Israel or with community and have little interest in ritual or Jewish learning; any combination of these themes is possible. Perhaps, though, the Torah seeks to convey that the fullness of the Jewish heritage is found by exploring and engaging with all of them.

Though this volume has focused on five central themes, there are abundant issues—from universalism and particularism to individual and collective responsibility; from family relationships, to war and peace, the environment, and more—raised in the Torah that are well worthy of further study. Living Torah is about the interpretation and application of Torah teachings in and by successive generations as part of an enduring aspiration to lead purposeful lives advancing the vision of a world repaired. It is participating in a continuing, life-encompassing conversation punctuated by action.

Some Jews have enjoyed the richest imaginable opportunities to engage with Torah in all of its breadth and depth. One such person, Emanuel Rackman, likely expressed the thoughts of many when he said: "I love being Jewish, living a Jewish life and sharing the past, present, and future of my people, because it is the best way I know to be truly human, truly a creature in the divine image. And what I love I want my offspring to have. It is the most valuable heritage I can bequeath to them. I am grateful to my parents that they gave it to me, and I pray that my loved ones will feel that way about me, precisely because I did for them what my parents did for me."[13]

Others, not born Jewish, have chosen to embrace Judaism. Over the years, I have had the opportunity to hear from many adults who have shared why they chose to become Jewish. Often, each of the five themes explored in these pages is referenced in the course of their remarks. These people are "Torah Jews."

Many born Jews have not had the opportunity to delve deeply into the Torah and its themes. They are occasional participants in the Jewish conversation or stand altogether outside it. In some cases, they might have encountered a very limited bit of Jewish learning as children and suppose that further engagement with Jewish texts and experience has little to offer.

Several years ago, I read an anecdote about a poor Russian Jew, circa 1880, who heard from his more affluent acquaintances that blintzes are delicious. Never having tasted a blintz, he asked his wife—the cook in the family—to prepare a meal of blintzes. "Blintzes," she replied, "Blintzes require eggs, and we have no eggs." "Skip the eggs, then," the blintz-curious husband suggested. "But blintzes require milk," said his pragmatic spouse. "Use water," proposed the husband. "But blintzes are filled with fruit, or cheese, or potatoes," said the incredulous wife, "and we have nothing with which to fill blintzes." "Skip the filling, then," replied the husband. "But blintzes are made with fine, sifted flour, and we have only coarse meal," said the wife. "Just make blintzes with the ingredients we have on hand," implored the husband. When, an hour later, the man tasted "blintzes" made of coarse flour and water, he exclaimed: "I don't understand what people find so appealing about blintzes!"

The same phenomenon attaches to Jewish education. Those who experience Jewish learning in its breadth and depth are likely to find the taste quite remarkable; those for whom Jewish education is an amalgam of insubstantial ingredients wonder at the significance that others attach to it. In the third decade of the twenty-first century, opportunities for meaningful engagement with Jewish learning and experience abound for children as well as adults.

The Torah text, with its multiple themes and interpretive layers, has captured the imagination of generations of Jews—of varying perspectives and with different understandings—throughout the generations. The starting point of a timeless tradition, Torah is a source of personal meaning to diverse readers who seriously explore it, each through the lens of their experience. I recall attending a synagogue service at which the weekly Torah portion described the measurements and construction of the tabernacle and some of its accoutrements. My eyes glazed over; those chapters did not seem particularly edifying to me. During a lull in the Torah reading, a person seated next to me remarked with great enthusiasm: "Don't you love these chapters? They are among my favorite passages of the Torah!"

The Torah has important things to say to each of us and, at various times in life—anchored in personal experiences—each reader approaches and relates to it differently. Though the text remains constant, the individual who engages with it is ever changing. The person who begins the Torah cycle anew is, in that respect, not the same person who encountered the text the prior year.

Reflecting, decades ago, on the alienation of Jewish youth from "establishment" institutions, Eliezer Berkovits questioned whether young Jews had ever truly encountered or experienced Judaism:

It is just possible that our youth is too intelligent to be impressed by a Jewish education that is chiefly geared to a farcical bar mitzvah ceremony which is to culminate in the vulgarity of an ostentatious party, that adds meaninglessness to the farce. It is just possible that our youth is too honest to be impressed by the lip-service to a Synagogue—or Temple—Judaism that has no effects on the life that Jews lead outside the synagogue and the temple. It is just possible that the kind of superficial pale ghost of Judaism that the American Jew has tried to communicate to his children deserves to be rejected. The tragedy, of course, is that this youth identify the inadequacy and failings of their elders with Jewishness; that they believe that the spiritual vacuum in the midst of which they grew up is characteristic of Judaism itself, whereas in reality it is the extent of the alienation of their elders from authentic Judaism. In truth, they are alienated from the farce that was left after the alienation of the parent generation from the heart and soul of Judaism.[14]

Berkovits avers that, though marking the milestone of "coming of age" as Jewish adults, *b'nai mitzvah* have, frequently, not meaningfully encountered Torah. In recent years, many congregations have very consciously reimagined the educational experiences surrounding *bar* and *bat mitzvah* to make this milestone an organic part of a more comprehensive Jewish journey. For adults who might never have enjoyed the opportunity of a meaningful encounter with Torah, the path to Jewish study and experience is always open. One of the most prominent of the sages, Rabbi Akiba, was illiterate until age forty; Moses, known in Jewish tradition as "Moshe *rabbeinu*"—Moses our teacher—began his career at age eighty.

Regardless of one's understanding of God—and the same person might well reflect upon or experience God's presence or absence differently, at different times—Torah, as interpreted and applied over scores of generations, has shaped the thoughts and actions of Jews throughout the world; it remains an enduring source of wisdom. Though this book is framed around the Pentateuch, the five books that are the first part of the Hebrew Bible, Torah, in its broadest sense, refers to the entire corpus of Jewish texts. I have drawn on interpretive literature from classical *midrashim* and Talmudic texts, medieval and modern commentaries, and contemporary expositors to explain aspects of the Pentateuch as understood, over time, as well as to serve as an introduction to further study.[15]

In a book titled *A Letter in the Scroll*, Jonathan Sacks invites us to imagine ourselves as browsers in a library:

Imagine that, while browsing in the library, you come across one book unlike the rest, which catches your eye because on its spine is written the name of your family. Intrigued you open it and see many pages written by different hands in many languages. You start reading it, and gradually you begin to understand what it is. It is the story each generation of your ancestors has told for the sake of the next, so that everyone born into this family can learn where they came from, what happened to them, what they lived for and why. As you turn the pages, you reach the last, which carries no entry but a heading. It bears your name. . . . Were I to find myself holding such a book in my hands, my life would already have been changed. Seeing my name and the story of my forebears, I could not read it as if it were just one story among others; instead, reading it would inevitably become, for me, a form of self-discovery. Once I knew that it existed, I could not put the book back on the shelf and forget it, because I would now know that I am part of a long line of people who traveled toward a certain destination and whose journey remains unfinished, dependent on me to take it further.[16]

For millennia, Jews have lived lives informed by the Torah. The commentaries referenced in this volume reflect understandings of Torah that have guided Jews in various times and places and convey accumulated wisdom to us, their legatees. Next chapters are for us to write.

Living at a time of considerable change, one of the teachers quoted in the Mishnah advises, "Turn it [Torah] and turn it over again, for everything is in it" (Avot 5:25). Explore all the angles of Torah, this teacher (Ben Bag Bag) counsels: it is a guide to all aspects of life. Ben Bag Bag's declaration is followed immediately by the comment of another sage: "According to the labor is the reward" (Avot 5:26). Serious engagement with Torah will enrich the life of the learner commensurate with the extent of investment in its study.

The Talmud relates that an individual once came before Hillel asking to learn the Torah while standing on one foot. Hillel responded: "What is hateful to you, do not do to your neighbor. That is the whole Torah, while the rest is commentary; go and learn it" (Shabbat 31a). For Jews in search of meaning, the Torah can be the starting point of a journey that has much to offer. Not only will the traveler find personal meaning, they will contribute to an enduring conversation—inspiring and accompanied by action—that continues to serve as a blessing to its participants and the world of which they are a part.

Notes

INTRODUCTION

1. Jonathan D. Sarna, *American Judaism: A History* (New Haven, CT: Yale University Press, 2004), 375.

2. Samson Raphael Hirsch, *The Nineteen Letters of Ben Uziel: Being a Spiritual Presentation of the Principles of Judaism*, trans. Bernard Drachman (New York: Funk and Wagnalls, 1899).

3. Milton Steinberg, *Basic Judaism* (New York: Harcourt Brace, 1947), ix–x.

4. Herman Wouk, *This Is My God* (Garden City, NY: Doubleday, 1959).

5. Dennis Prager and Joseph Telushkin, *Eight Questions People Ask about Judaism* (Simi Valley, CA: Tze Ulmad Press, 1975).

6. David Wolpe, *Why Be Jewish?* (New York: Henry Holt, 1995).

7. Among the more recent such books encouraging readers to find personal meaning in Judaism are Roberta Rosenthal Kwall, *Remix Judaism: Preserving Tradition in a Diverse World* (Lanham, MD: Rowman & Littlefield, 2020), and Zack Bodner, *Why Do Jewish?* (Jerusalem: Gefen, 2022).

8. Those interested in exploring contemporary research relating to the development of the Hebrew Bible, with particular attention to the Torah text, can find an outstanding book on this subject by (Jewish) Bible scholar and longtime Harvard University professor James L. Kugel, *How to Read the Bible: A Guide to Scripture, Then and Now* (New York: Free Press, 2007). In this scholarly yet accessible work of eight-hundred-plus pages, Kugel makes the point that whatever the circumstances of the Torah's composition, it is the interpretation of the text that establishes its enduring meaning. "The written text alone is not all-powerful; in fact, it rarely stands on its own. Its true significance usually

lies not in the plain sense of its words but in what the Oral Torah has made of those words" (681).

9. Jonathan Sacks, *A Letter in the Scroll* (New York: Simon and Schuster, 2000), 173.

10. Ibid., 164–65.

11. Jonathan Sacks, *Morality* (New York: Basic Books, 2020).

12. Jonathan Sacks, *Lessons in Leadership* (New Milford, CT: Maggid, 2015), 14–15.

CHAPTER 1

1. Jonathan Sacks, *Celebrating Life* (London: Bloomsbury Continuum, 2021), 83.

2. Abraham J. Heschel, *Who Is Man?* (Stanford, CA: Stanford University Press, 1965), 78–79.

3. Sacks, *A Letter in the Scroll*, 173.

4. Nahum Sarna, *Understanding Genesis* (New York: Schocken, 1972), xxiii.

5. Elliot N. Dorff, *The Way into Tikkun Olam* (Woodstock, VT: Jewish Lights, 2007), 14.

6. Nahum Sarna, *Genesis* (Philadelphia: Jewish Publication Society, 1989), 119.

7. Ethan Tucker, "Redeeming the *Akeidah*, *Halakhah*, and Ourselves" (New York: Hadar Institute, Center for Jewish Law and Values, 2015), 22.

8. Sarna, *Understanding Genesis*, 184.

CHAPTER 2

1. Micah Goodman, *The Wondering Jew*, trans. Eylon Levy (New Haven, CT: Yale University Press, 2020), 91–92.

2. Marc Zvi Brettler, *How to Read the Bible* (Philadelphia: Jewish Publication Society, 2005), 280.

3. Goodman, *The Wondering Jew*, 87.

4. Emanuel Rackman, *A Modern Orthodox Life* (Jersey City, NJ: Ktav, 2008), 172.

5. A Statement of Principles for Reform Judaism: Adopted in Pittsburgh—1999, ccarnet.org/rabbinic-voice/platforms/article-statement-principles-reform-Judaism/.

6. Milton Steinberg, *Basic Judaism* (New York: Harcourt Brace, 1947), 39.

7. Tamar Ross, *Expanding the Palace of Torah: Orthodoxy and Feminism* (Waltham, MA: Brandeis University Press, 2004), 129.

8. David J. Wolpe, *Teaching Your Children about God* (New York: Henry Holt, 1993), 14.

9. Harold M. Schulweis, *For Those Who Can't Believe: Overcoming the Obstacles to Faith* (New York: HarperCollins, 1994), 136.

10. For an outstanding work on Zionism and its relationship to the messianic idea in Judaism as understood within religious circles, see Avi Ravitsky, *Messianism, Zionism, and Jewish Religious Radicalism*, trans. Michael Swirsky, and Jonathan Chipman (Chicago: University of Chicago Press, 1996).

11. Martin Gilbert, *Israel: A History* (New York: William Morrow and Co., Inc., 1998), 47.

12. Ibid., 255.

13. Ibid., 344.

14. See, in particular, Arthur Hertzberg, *The Zionist Idea* (Philadelphia: Jewish Publication Society, 1997).

15. Louis Brandeis, "The Jewish Problem: How to Solve It" (New York: The Zionist Essays Publication Committee, 1915), 12–13.

16. The Jewish Agency for Israel, "Jewish Population Rises to 15.7 Million Worldwide in 2023," https://www.jewishagency.org/jewish-population-rises-to-15-7-million-worldwide-in-2023/. These data are drawn from the work of noted demographer Sergio Della Pergola who estimates that 13.5 million of the world's 15.7 million Jews live in Israel or the United States. Professor Della Pergola's Jewish population estimates refer to individuals identifying themselves as Jews by religion or otherwise and who do not identify with another religion.

17. Pew Research Center, "Jewish Americans in 2020," May 11, 2021, 50.

18. Jewish Virtual Library, "Jewish & Non-Jewish Population of Israel/Palestine (1517–Present)," https://www.jewishvirtuallibrary.org/jewish-and-non-jewish-population-of-israel-palestine-1517-present.

19. For a nuanced look at the question, "Seventy-five years after its creation, has Israel fulfilled its founders' dreams?" see Daniel Gordis, *Impossible Takes Longer* (New York: Harper Collins, 2023).

CHAPTER 3

1. Jonathan Sacks, "History and Memory," in *Rabbi Jonathan Sacks's Haggadah* (New York: Continuum, 2007), 30.

2. Nahum Sarna, *Exploring Exodus: The Origins of Biblical Israel* (New York: Schocken, 1996), xix.

3. Ibid., 7.

4. Jonathan Sacks, "The Omer and the Politics of Torah," in *Rabbi Jonathan Sacks's Haggadah* (New York: Continuum, 2007), 68.

5. David Hartman, *A Living Covenant: The Innovative Spirit in Traditional Judaism* (New York: Macmillan, 1985), 8.

6. Marc Z. Brettler, *How to Read the Jewish Bible* (New York: Oxford University Press, 2007), 24.

7. Irving Greenberg, *The Jewish Way: Living the Holidays* (New York: Simon and Schuster, 1988), 25.

8. Sarna, *Exploring Exodus*, 25.

9. Nehama Leibowitz, *Studies in Shemot*, Part 1 (Jerusalem: Jewish Agency, 1986), 95.

10. Sarna, *Exploring Exodus*, 64.

11. Schulweis, *For Those Who Can't Believe*, 49.

12. Elisheva Carlebach, *Palaces of Time: Jewish Calendar and Culture in Early Modern Europe* (Cambridge, MA: Harvard University Press, 2011), 5.

13. David Hartman, *A Living Covenant*, 261.

14. Sarna, *Exploring Exodus*, 119.

15. See, in this connection, Shai Held, *The Heart of Torah: Essays on the Weekly Torah Portion—Genesis and Exodus*, Vol 1 (Philadelphia: Jewish Publication Society, 2017), 165–68.

16. Jonathan Sacks, *The Dignity of Difference* (London: Bloomsbury, 2003), 135.

17. Sarna, *Exploring Exodus*, 144.

18. Ibid., 142.

19. On rabbinic approaches to the human factor in revelation, see David Weiss Halivni, "On Man's Role in Revelation," in *From Ancient Israel to Modern Judaism*, Vol. 2, ed. Jacob Neusner et al. (Atlanta: Scholar's Press, 1989), 29–49. For a comprehensive look at the broad range of approaches to the development of Oral Law see Jay M. Harris, *How Do We Know This? Midrash and the Fragmentation of Modern Judaism* (Albany: State University of New York, 1995).

20. Elliot N. Dorff and Arthur Rosett, *A Living Tree: The Roots and Growth of Jewish Law* (Albany: State University of New York, 1988), 198.

21. Louis Jacobs, *A Jewish Theology* (New York: Behrman House, 1973), 207.

22. Samson Raphael Hirsch, *The Pentateuch: Translation and Commentary*, Exodus, trans. Isaac Levy (Gateshead: Judaica Press, 1976), 428–29.

23. Sarna, *Exploring Exodus*, 200.

24. Ibid., 209.

25. Ibid., 214.

CHAPTER 4

1. Steinberg, *Basic Judaism*, 47.

2. Will Herberg, *Judaism and Modern Man* (New York: Atheneum, 1973), 193–94.

3. Jonathan Sacks, "Time as a Narrative of Hope," in *Rabbi Jonathan Sacks's Haggadah* (New York: Continuum, 2007), 76–77.

4. Sacks, "History and Memory," 30.

5. David L. Lieber, "The Covenant and the Election of Israel," in *Etz Hayim: Torah and Commentary*, ed. David L. Lieber (Philadelphia: Jewish Publication Society, 2001), 1418.

6. David Hartman, *A Living Covenant*, 261.

7. Sacks, "Time as a Narrative of Hope," 79.

8. Tamar Ross, "Divine Hiddenness and Human Input: The Potential Contribution of a Postmodern View of Revelation to Yitz Greenberg's Holocaust Theology," in *Yitz Greenberg and Modern Orthodoxy* (Boston: Academic Studies Press, 2019), 112–13.

9. Eliezer Berkovits, *Not in Heaven: The Nature and Function of Halakha* (New York: Ktav, 1983), 1.

10. Emanuel Rackman, "Meta-Halacha Values," *Justice* 16 (1998). On Berkovits's and Rackman's values-conscious approach to *halakhah*, see Gil Graff, "Halakhah as *Torat Hayyim*: The Values-Conscious Visions of Eliezer Berkovits and Emanuel Rackman," *Journal of Modern Jewish Studies* 18, no. 3 (2019): 330–42.

11. Ross, *Expanding the Palace of Torah*, 222.

12. Ibid., 63–64.

13. Ibid., 223.

14. Donniel Hartman, *Putting God Second: How to Save Religion from Itself* (Boston: Beacon Press, 2016), 117.

15. Sacks, "Time as a Narrative of Hope," 80–81.

16. Sacks, *The Dignity of Difference*, 94.

17. Yosef Hayim Yerushalmi, *Zakhor: Jewish History and Jewish Memory* (Seattle: University of Washington Press, 1996), 9.

18. Stephen Carter, *Civility: Manners, Morals, and the Etiquette of Democracy* (New York: Harper Perennial, 1999), 62, 71, 75.

CHAPTER 5

1. Gordon Tucker, "Sacrifices," in *Etz Hayim: Torah and Commentary*, ed. David L. Lieber (Philadelphia: Jewish Publication Society, 2001), 1447.

2. Jacob Milgrom, *Leviticus: A Book of Ritual and Ethics* (Minneapolis: Fortress Press, 2005), 22.

3. Micah Goodman, *Maimonides and the Book That Changed Judaism*, trans. Yedidya Sinclair (Philadelphia: Jewish Publication Society, 2015), 129.

4. Nehama Leibowitz, *Studies in Vayikra* (Jerusalem: Jewish Agency, 1985), 22.

5. Shai Held, *The Heart of Torah: Essays on the Weekly Torah Portion— Leviticus, Numbers, and Deuteronomy*, Vol. 2 (Philadelphia: Jewish Publication Society, 2017), 11.

6. Samson Raphael Hirsch, *The Pentateuch: Translation and Commentary*, Leviticus, Vol. 1, 254.

7. Milgrom, *Leviticus*, 107.

8. Jonathan Klawans, "Concepts of Purity in the Bible," in *Jewish Study Bible*, ed. Adele Berlin and Mark Z. Brettler (Oxford: Oxford University Press, 2004), 2042.

9. Baruch J. Schwartz, Commentary on Leviticus, in *Jewish Study Bible*, ed. Adele Berlin and Mark Z. Brettler (Oxford: Oxford University Press, 2004), 232.

10. Held, *The Heart of Torah*, Vol. 2, 41.

11. Hirsch, *The Pentateuch*, Leviticus, Vol. 2, 422.

12. Milgrom, *Leviticus*, 209.

13. Leibowitz, *Studies in Vaykra*, 168.

14. Milgrom, *Leviticus*, 212.

15. Hirsch, *The Pentateuch*, Leviticus, Vol. 2, 510.

CHAPTER 6

1. Daniel Gordis, *God Was Not in the Fire* (New York: Scribner, 1995), 109.

2. Abraham Joshua Heschel, *Man's Quest for God* (New York: Charles Scribner's Sons, 1954), 7.

3. Ibid., 63–64.

4. Ibid., 64–65.

5. The Hebrew *emunatekha* readily lends itself to this reading. It is, however, more commonly translated as "great is Your faithfulness."

6. Samson Raphael Hirsch, *The Hirsch Haggadah* (New York: Feldheim, 1993), 50–51.

7. I. Greenberg, *The Jewish Way*, 24.

8. Jeffrey Fox, *Gay Women (Nashim Mesolelot): A Teshuva* (New York: Yeshivat Maharat, 2023), 78.

9. Tamar Ross, "Behind Every Revelation Lurks an Interpretation: Revisiting 'The Revelation at Sinai,'" May 2, 2023, Thelehrhaus.com/scholarship/behind-every-revelation-lurks-an-interpretation-revisiting-the-revelation-at-sinai.

10. Ephraim Mirvis, *The Wellbeing of LGBT+ Pupils: A Guide for Orthodox Jewish Schools* (London: Office of the Chief Rabbi, 2018), 3.

11. Ibid., 11.

12. For a summary of Conservative movement *responsa* relating to homosexuality, see Elliot N. Dorff, *Modern Conservative Judaism: Evolving Thought and Practice* (Lincoln, NE: Jewish Publication Society, 2018), 287–301. The Reform movement has affirmed that same-sex marriages can be consecrated as *kiddushin*, the traditional term for Jewish marriage. CCAR Responsa Committee—2014, 5774.4: Same-Sex Marriage as Kiddushin, https://www.ccarnet.org/ccar-responsa/same-sex-marriage-kiddushin/.

13. Abraham Joshua Heschel, *The Sabbath: Its Meaning for Modern Man* (New York: Farrar, Straus and Young, 1951), 29.

14. I. Greenberg, *The Jewish Way*, 65.

15. Ibid., 22.

16. For a look at the historic and contemporary meaning of the cycle of Jewish holidays—including postbiblical holidays—see I. Greenberg, *The Jewish Way*.

CHAPTER 7

1. Jacob Milgrom, *Numbers* (Commentary) (Philadelphia: Jewish Publication Society, 1990), 350.

2. Samson Raphael Hirsch, *The Pentateuch: Translation and Commentary*, Numbers, 77.

3. Nehama Leibowitz, *Studies in Bamidbar* (Jerusalem, World Zionist Organization, 1982), 67.

4. Milgrom, *Numbers*, 361.

5. Leibowitz, *Studies in Bamidbar*, 78.

6. Held, *The Heart of Torah*, Vol. 2, 95.

7. Ibid., 97.

8. Hirsch, *The Pentateuch*, Numbers, 185.

9. Held, *The Heart of Torah*, Vol. 2, 118.

10. Leibowitz, *Studies in Bamidbar*, 146.

11. Ibid., 181.

12. Ibid., 326.

13. Milgrom, *Numbers*, 216.

14. Ibid., 250.

15. Held, *The Heart of Torah*, Vol. 2, 190.
16. Milgrom, *Numbers*, 291.
17. Held, *The Heart of Torah*, Vol. 2, 193–94.

CHAPTER 8

1. Shaye J. D. Cohen, *The Beginnings of Jewishness* (Berkeley: University of California Press, 1999), 7.
2. David Hartman, *A Heart of Many Rooms* (Nashville, TN: Jewish Lights, 2015), 51.
3. David Biale, ed., *Cultures of the Jews* (New York: Schocken, 2002), xxiv–xxv.
4. Heschel, *Man's Quest for God*, 46.
5. Lee I. Levine, *The Ancient Synagogue: The First Thousand Years* (New Haven, CT: Yale University Press, 2000), 1.
6. Ibid., 4.
7. Ibid., 501.
8. Ibid., 606.
9. Mordecai Kaplan, *Judaism as a Civilization: Toward a Reconstruction of American-Jewish Life* (New York: Macmillan, 1934).
10. Steven M. Cohen and Arnold Eisen, *The Jew Within: Self, Family, and Community in America* (Bloomington: Indiana University Press, 2000), 7.
11. Jonathan Woocher, "Building Community and Peoplehood in a Time of Personalism," July 6, 2008, retrieved from https://ejewishphilanthropy.com/building-community-and-peoplehood-in-a-time-of-personalism/.
12. Jonathan Krasner, "Jonathan Woocher and the Imperative of Jewish Community in the Age of the Sovereign Self," in *Where Jewish Education Helps Students Thrive: A Tribute to Dr. Jonathan Woocher* (New York: The Jewish Federations of North America and The Jewish Education Project, 2018), 48.
13. Cohen, *The Beginnings of Jewishness*, 346.
14. Ibid., 347.
15. Milton Steinberg, *A Partisan Guide to the Jewish Problem* (New York: Bobbs-Merrill, 1945), 151.
16. Donniel Hartman, *Putting God Second*, 137.

CHAPTER 9

1. Jeffrey H. Tigay, *Deuteronomy* (Commentary) (Philadelphia: Jewish Publication Society, 1996), xviii.

2. Held, *The Heart of Torah*, Vol. 2, 203.

3. Nehama Leibowitz, *Studies in Devarim* (Jerusalem: Jewish Agency, 1982), 28.

4. Tigay, *Deuteronomy*, 46.

5. Leibowitz, *Studies in Devarim*, 63.

6. Tigay, *Deuteronomy*, 122.

7. Ibid., 166.

8. Held, *The Heart of Torah*, Vol. 2, 249.

9. Leibowitz, *Studies in Devarim*, 207.

10. Held, *The Heart of Torah*, Vol. 2, 238.

11. Ibid., 238–39.

12. Ibid., 264.

13. Ibid., 279.

14. Ibid., 289.

15. Sacks, *A Letter in the Scroll*, 34.

CHAPTER 10

1. Quoted in *A History of the Jewish People*, ed. H. H. Ben-Sasson (Cambridge, MA: Harvard University Press, 1976), 522.

2. Jonathan Woocher, "Reinventing Jewish Education for the 21st Century." *Journal of Jewish Education* 78, no. 3 (2012): 218.

3. Gordis, *God Was Not in the Fire*, 94.

4. Moshe Greenberg, "We Were as Those Who Dream: An Agenda for an Ideal Jewish Education," in *Visions of Jewish Education*, ed. Seymour Fox, Israel Schaffler, and Daniel Marom (Cambridge: Cambridge University Press, 2003), 123.

5. From *Emet Ve-Emunah: Statement of Principles of Conservative Judaism* (1988). Quoted in Dorff, *Modern Conservative Judaism*, 85.

6. Gordis, *God Was Not in the Fire*, 223.

7. Central Conference of American Rabbis, "A Statement of Principles for Reform Judaism: Adopted in Pittsburgh-1999." ccarnet.org/rabbinic-voice/platforms/article-statement-principles-reform-Judaism/.

8. Dorff, *Modern Conservative Judaism*, 91.

9. Michael A. Meyer, "Reflections on the Educated Jew from the Perspective of Reform Judaism," in *Visions of Jewish Education*, ed. Fox et al., 157.

10. Jonathan Sacks, *The Great Partnership: Science, Religion, and the Search for Meaning* (New York: Schocken, 2011), 294.

11. Ibid., 37.

12. Heschel, *Man's Quest for God*, 109.

13. Rackman, *A Modern Orthodox Life*, 120.

14. Eliezer Berkovits, "Between Yesterday and Tomorrow," address delivered at the annual dinner of the Chicago Academy Associates, circa 1970, pp. 4–5. A copy of this address is among documents maintained in Israel by Professor Avraham Berkovits, eldest son of Eliezer Berkovits, who graciously provided access to his father's collected papers.

15. For those interested in looking at contemporary commentary on the weekly Torah portion, two—among many—websites that regularly post such commentary are https://www.hadar.org/torah-tefillah/torah-portions and https://www.thetorah.com. The latter site features contributions by individuals in the academic field of biblical studies who seek to bridge the worlds of critical scholarship and religious faith. The two-volume work by Shai Held, *The Heart of Torah*, referenced in this volume (see bibliography) offers insightful commentary. Its author is among the heads of the Hadar Institute, which provides an array of opportunities—in person and online—for studying classical Jewish texts. A recent publication organized by the weekly Torah portion uniquely focuses on the many questions asked within the Torah (for example, Pharaoh asks Moses, "Who is the Lord that I should heed Him and let Israel go?" and Moses asks the Gadites and Reubenites, "Are your brothers to go to war while you stay here?"). The author explores the significance of the hundreds of such questions that appear within the Torah text with an eye to lessons for contemporary readers. Joshua Hoffman, *The Holiness of Doubt: A Journey through the Questions of the Torah* (Lanham, MD: Rowman & Littlefield, 2023).

16. Sacks, *A Letter in the Scroll*, 43–44.

Bibliography

Ben-Sasson, H. H., ed. *A History of the Jewish People*. Cambridge, MA: Harvard University Press, 1976.

Berkovits, Eliezer. "Between Yesterday and Tomorrow." Berkovits Papers (circa 1970): 9 pages.

———. *Not in Heaven: The Nature and Function of Halakha.* New York: Ktav, 1983.

Biale, David, ed. *Cultures of the Jews*. New York: Schocken, 2002.

Bodner, Zack. *Why Do Jewish?* Jerusalem: Gefen, 2022.

Brandeis, Louis. "The Jewish Problem: How to Solve It." New York: The Zionist Essays Publication Committee, 1915.

Brettler, Marc Z. *How to Read the Bible*. Philadelphia: Jewish Publication Society, 2005.

———. *How to Read the Jewish Bible*. New York: Oxford University Press, 2007.

Carlebach, Elisheva. *Palaces of Time: Jewish Calendar and Culture in Early Modern Europe*. Cambridge, MA: Harvard University Press, 2011.

Carter, Stephen. *Civility: Manners, Morals, and the Etiquette of Democracy*. New York: Harper Perennial, 1999.

CCAR Responsa Committee. "Same-Sex Marriage as Kiddushin." 2014-5774.4. ccarnet.org/ccar-responsa/same-sex/marriage-kiddushin/.

Central Conference of American Rabbis. "A Statement of Principles for Reform Judaism: Adopted in Pittsburgh-1999." ccarnet.org/rabbinic-voice/platforms/article-statement-principles-reform-Judaism/.

Cohen, Shaye J. D. *The Beginnings of Jewishness*. Berkeley: University of California Press, 1999.

Cohen, Steven M., and Arnold Eisen. *The Jew Within: Self, Family, and Community in America*. Bloomington: Indiana University Press, 2000.

Dorff, Elliot N. *Modern Conservative Judaism: Evolving Thought and Practice*. Lincoln, NE: Jewish Publication Society, 2018.

———. *The Way into Tikkun Olam.* Woodstock, VT: Jewish Lights, 2007.

Dorff, Elliot N., and Arthur Rosett. *A Living Tree: The Roots and Growth of Jewish Law.* Albany: State University of New York, 1988.

Fox, Jeffrey. *Gay Women (Nashim Mesolelot): A Teshuva.* New York: Yeshivat Maharat, 2023.

Gilbert, Martin. *Israel: A History.* New York: William Morrow and Co., Inc., 1998.

Goodman, Micah. *Maimonides and the Book That Changed Judaism.* Translated by Yedidya Sinclair. Philadelphia: Jewish Publication Society, 2015.

———. *The Wondering Jew.* Translated by Eylon Levy. New Haven, CT: Yale University Press, 2020.

Gordis, Daniel. *God Was Not in the Fire.* New York: Scribner, 1995.

———. *Impossible Takes Longer.* New York: HarperCollins, 2023.

Graff, Gil. "Halakhah as *Torat Hayyim*: The Values-Conscious Visions of Eliezer Berkovits and Emanuel Rackman." *Journal of Modern Jewish Studies* 18, no. 3 (2019): 330–42.

Greenberg, Irving. *The Jewish Way: Living the Holidays.* New York: Simon and Schuster, 1988.

Greenberg, Moshe. "We Were as Those Who Dream: An Agenda for an Ideal Jewish Education." In *Visions of Jewish Education*, ed. Seymour Fox, Israel Scheffler, and Daniel Marom, 122–32. Cambridge: Cambridge University Press, 2003.

Harris, Jay M. *How Do We Know This? Midrash and the Fragmentation of Modern Judaism.* Albany: State University of New York, 1995.

Hartman, David. *A Heart of Many Rooms.* Nashville, TN: Jewish Lights, 2015.

———. *A Living Covenant: The Innovative Spirit in Traditional Judaism.* New York: Macmillan, 1985.

Hartman, Donniel. *Putting God Second: How to Save Religion from Itself.* Boston: Beacon Press, 2016.

Held, Shai. *The Heart of Torah: Essays on the Weekly Torah Portion—Genesis and Exodus, Vol. 1.* Philadelphia: Jewish Publication Society, 2017.

———. *The Heart of Torah: Essays on the Weekly Torah Portion—Leviticus, Numbers and Deuteronomy, Vol 2.* Philadelphia: Jewish Publication Society, 2017.

Herberg, Will. *Judaism and Modern Man.* New York: Athenum, 1973.

Hertzberg, Arthur. *The Zionist Idea.* Philadelphia: Jewish Publication Society, 1997.

Heschel, Abraham J. *Man's Quest for God.* New York: Charles Scribner's Sons, 1954.

———. *The Sabbath: Its Meaning for Modern Man.* New York: Farrar, Straus and Young, 1951.

———. *Who Is Man?* Stanford, CA: Stanford University Press, 1965.

Hirsch, Samson Raphael. *The Hirsch Haggadah*. New York: Feldheim, 1993.
———. *The Nineteen Letters of Ben Uziel*. Translated by Bernard Drachman. New York: Funk and Wagnalls, 1899.
———. *The Pentateuch: Translation and Commentary*. Translated by Isaac Levy. Gateshead: Judaica Press, 1976.
Hoffman, Joshua. *The Holiness of Doubt: A Journey through the Questions of the Torah*. Lanham, MD: Rowman & Littlefield, 2023.
Jacobs, Louis. *A Jewish Theology*. New York: Behrman House, 1973.
The Jewish Agency for Israel. "Jewish Population Rises to 15.7 Million Worldwide in 2023." https://www.jewishagency.org/jewish-population-rises -to-15-7-million-worldwide-in-2023/.
Jewish Virtual Library. "Jewish & Non-Jewish Population of Israel/Palestine (1517–Present). https://www.jewishvirtuallibrary.org/jewish-and-non-jewish -population-of-israel-palestine-1517-present/.
Kaplan, Mordecai. *Judaism as a Civilization: Toward a Reconstruction of American-Jewish Life*. New York: Macmillan, 1934.
Klawans, Jonathan. "Concepts of Purity in the Bible." In *Jewish Study Bible*, ed. Adele Berlin and Marc Z. Brettler, 2041–47. Oxford: Oxford University Press, 2004.
Krasner, Jonathan. "Jonathan Woocher and the Imperative of Jewish Community in the Age of the Sovereign Self." In *Where Jewish Education Helps Students Thrive: A Tribute to Dr. Jonathan Woocher*, 42–50. New York: The Jewish Federations of North America and the Jewish Education Project, 2018.
Kugel, James L. *How to Read the Bible: A Guide to Scripture, Then and Now*. New York: Free Press, 2007.
Kwall, Roberta Rosenthal. *Remix Judaism: Preserving Tradition in a Diverse World*. Lanham, MD: Rowman & Littlefield, 2020.
Leibowitz, Nehama. *Studies in Bamidbar*. Jerusalem: World Zionist Organization, 1982.
———. *Studies in Devarim*. Jerusalem: World Zionist Organization, 1982.
———. *Studies in Shemot*, Part I. Jerusalem: World Zionist Organization, 1986.
———. *Studies in Vayikra*. Jerusalem: World Zionist Organization, 1985.
Levine, Lee I. *The Ancient Synagogue: The First Thousand Years*. New Haven, CT: Yale University Press, 2000.
Lieber, David L. "The Covenant and the Election of Israel." In *Etz Hayim: Torah and Commentary*, ed. David L. Lieber, 1416–20. Philadelphia: Jewish Publication Society, 2001.
Meyer, Michael A. "Reflections on the Educated Jew from the Perspective of Reform Judaism." In *Visions of Jewish Education*, ed. Seymour Fox et al., 149–61.
Milgrom, Jacob. *Leviticus: A Book of Ritual and Ethics*. Minneapolis: Fortress Press, 2005.

———. *Numbers* (Commentary). Philadelphia: Jewish Publication Society, 1990.

Mirvis, Ephraim. *The Well-being of LGBT+ Pupils: A Guide for Orthodox Jewish Schools.* London: Office of the Chief Rabbi, 2018.

Pew Research Center. "Jewish Americans in 2020." May 11, 2021.

Prager, Dennis, and Joseph Telushkin. *Eight Questions People Ask about Judaism.* Simi Valley, CA: Tze Ulmad Press, 1975.

Rackman, Emanuel. "Meta-Halacha Values." *Justice* 16 (March 1998): 39–42.

———. *A Modern Orthodox Life.* Jersey City, NJ: Ktav, 2008.

Ravitsky, Aviezer. *Messianism, Zionism, and Jewish Religious Radicalism.* Translated by Michael Swirsky and Jonathan Chipman. Chicago: University of Chicago Press, 1996.

Ross, Tamar. "Behind Every Revelation Lurks an Interpretation: Revisiting 'The Revelation at Sinai.'" May 2, 2023. Thelehrhaus.com/scholarship /behind-every-revelation-lurks-an-interpretation-revisiting-the-revelation-at-sinai/.

———. "Divine Hiddenness and Human Input: The Potential Contribution of a Postmodern View of Revelation to Yitz Greenberg's Holocaust Theology." In *Yitz Greenberg and Modern Orthodoxy*, ed. Adam S. Ferziger, Miri Freud-Kandel, and Steven Bayme, 107–28. Boston: Academic Studies Press, 2019.

———. *Expanding the Palace of Torah: Orthodoxy and Feminism.* Waltham, MA: Brandeis University Press, 2004.

Sacks, Jonathan. *Celebrating Life.* London: Bloomsbury Continuum, 2021.

———. *The Dignity of Difference.* London: Bloomsbury, 2003.

———. *The Great Partnership: Science, Religion, and the Search for Meaning.* New York: Schocken, 2011.

———. "History and Memory." In *Rabbi Jonathan Sacks's Haggadah*, 27–31. New York: Continuum, 2007.

———. *Lessons in Leadership.* New Milford, CT: Maggid, 2015.

———. *A Letter in the Scroll.* New York: Simon and Schuster, 2000.

———. *Morality.* New York: Basic Books, 2020.

———. "The Omer and the Politics of Torah." In *Rabbi Jonathan Sacks's Haggadah*, 67–74. New York: Continuum, 2007.

———. "Time as a Narrative of Hope." In *Rabbi Jonathan Sacks's Haggadah*, 75–83. New York: Continuum, 2007.

Sarna, Jonathan D. *American Judaism: A History.* New Haven, CT: Yale University Press, 2004.

Sarna, Nahum. *Exploring Exodus: The Origins of Biblical Israel.* New York: Schocken, 1996.

———. *Genesis* (Commentary). Philadelphia: Jewish Publication Society, 1989.

———. *Understanding Genesis.* New York: Schocken, 1972.

Schulweis, Harold M. *For Those Who Can't Believe: Overcoming the Obstacles to Faith*. New York: HarperCollins, 1994.

Schwartz, Baruch J. Commentary on Leviticus. In *Jewish Study Bible*, ed. Adele Berlin and Marc Z. Brettler. Oxford: Oxford University Press, 2004.

Steinberg, Milton. *Basic Judaism*. New York: Harcourt Brace, 1947.

———. *A Partisan Guide to the Jewish Problem*. New York: Bobbs-Merrill, 1945.

Tigay, Jeffrey H. *Deuteronomy* (Commentary). Philadelphia: Jewish Publication Society, 1996.

Tucker, Ethan. "Redeeming the *Akeidah, Halakhah*, and Ourselves." New York: Hadar Institute, Center for Jewish Law and Values, 2015.

Tucker, Gordon. "Sacrifices." In *Etz Hayim: Torah and Commentary*, ed. David L. Lieber, 1446–50. Philadelphia: Jewish Publication Society, 2001.

Weiss, David Halivni. "On Man's Role in Revelation." In *From Ancient Israel to Modern Judaism*, Vol. 2, ed. Jacob Neusner et al., 29–49. Atlanta: Scholar's Press, 1989.

Wolpe, David J. *Teaching Your Children About God*. New York: Henry Holt, 1993.

———. *Why Be Jewish?* New York: Henry Holt, 1995.

Woocher, Jonathan. "Building Community and Peoplehood in a Time of Personalism." July 6, 2008. https://ejewishphilanthropy.com/building-community-and-peoplehood-in-a-time-of-personalism/.

———. "Reinventing Jewish Education for the 21st Century." *Journal of Jewish Education* 78, no. 3 (2012): 182–226.

Wouk, Herman. *This Is My God*. Garden City, NY: Doubleday, 1959.

Wurzburger, Walter. *Ethics of Responsibility: Pluralistic Approaches to Convenantal Ethics*. Philadelphia: Jewish Publication Society, 1994.

Yerushalmi, Yosef Hayim. *Zakhor: Jewish History and Jewish Memory*. Seattle: University of Washington Press, 1996.

Index

About the Author

Gil Graff is an educator and earned his PhD in Jewish history and JD from UCLA. He holds master's degrees in history, Jewish studies, and educational administration. Since 1993 he has been executive director of Builders of Jewish Education (BJE), a nonprofit serving schools and students of all streams of Jewish life. Graff has served as an adjunct faculty member at the Academy for Jewish Religion California, American Jewish University, Spertus Institute for Jewish Learning and Leadership (Chicago), Touro College (Los Angeles), and the Rhea Hirsch School of Education (Hebrew Union College, Los Angeles). Earlier in his career, he was a teacher and school administrator.

Graff has authored over twenty articles that have appeared in scholarly publications. He has also written three books: *Jewish Tradition in a Western Key: Essays on Jews and Judaism in a Changing World, 1789–1939* (2019); *"And You Shall Teach Them Diligently": A Concise History of Jewish Education in the United States, 1776–2000* (2008); and *Separation of Church and State: Dina de-Malkhuta Dina in Jewish Law, 1750–1848* (1985).